PEOPLE
IN THE NEWS

Will Smith

by Marilyn D. Anderson

**LUCENT
BOOKS** ®

THOMSON
™
GALE

San Diego • Detroit • New York • San Francisco • Cleveland
New Haven, Conn. • Waterville, Maine • London • Munich

Titles in the People in the News series include:

Tim Allen	George Lucas
Drew Barrymore	Madonna
Tony Blair	Rosie O'Donnell
Garth Brooks	Brad Pitt
George W. Bush	Colin Powell
Jim Carrey	Princess Diana
Michael Crichton	Prince William
Matt Damon	Christopher Reeve
Celine Dion	Julia Roberts
Michael J. Fox	The Rolling Stones
Bill Gates	J.K. Rowling
Mel Gibson	Steven Spielberg
John Grisham	R.L. Stine
Jesse Jackson	Sting
Michael Jackson	John Travolta
Michael Jordan	Oprah Winfrey
Stephen King	Tiger Woods

LIBRARY OF CONGRESS CATALOGING-IN-PUBLICATION DATA

Anderson, Marilyn D.
 Will Smith / by Marilyn D. Anderson.
  p. cm. —— (People in the news)
 Includes bibliographical references and index.
  Summary: Actor and rap star Will Smith is profiled. The book discusses his life as a child and teen, his career paths in music and acting, and his life as a family man.
  ISBN 1-59018-140-9 (hardback : alk. paper)
 1. Smith, Will, 1968– Juvenile literature. 2. Actors——United States——Biography——Juvenile literature. 3. Rap musicians——United States——Biography——Juvenile literature. I. Title. II. People in the news (San Diego, Calif.)
 PN2287.S612 A54 2003
 791.43'028'092——dc21

                                            2002003589

Table of Contents

Foreword

FAME AND CELEBRITY are alluring. People are drawn to those who walk in fame's spotlight, whether they are known for great accomplishments or for notorious deeds. The lives of the famous pique public interest and attract attention, perhaps because their experiences seem in some ways so different from, yet in other ways so similar to, our own.

Newspapers, magazines, and television regularly capitalize on this fascination with celebrity by running profiles of famous people. For example, television programs such as *Entertainment Tonight* devote all of their programming to stories about entertainment and entertainers. Magazines such as *People* fill their pages with stories of the private lives of famous people. Even newspapers, newsmagazines, and television news frequently delve into the lives of well-known personalities. Despite the number of articles and programs, few provide more than a superficial glimpse at their subjects.

Lucent's People in the News series offers young readers a deeper look into the lives of today's newsmakers, the influences that have shaped them, and the impact they have had in their fields of endeavor and on other people's lives. The subjects of the series hail from many disciplines and walks of life. They include authors, musicians, athletes, political leaders, entertainers, entrepreneurs, and others who have made a mark on modern life and who, in many cases, will continue to do so for years to come.

These biographies are more than factual chronicles. Each book emphasizes the contributions, accomplishments, or deeds that have brought fame or notoriety to the individual and shows how that person has influenced modern life. Authors portray their subjects in a realistic, unsentimental light. For example, Bill Gates—the cofounder and chief executive officer of the software giant Microsoft—has been instrumental in making personal computers the most vital tool of the modern age. Few dispute his business savvy, his perseverance, or his technical expertise, yet critics say he is ruthless in his dealings with competitors and driven more by his desire to maintain Microsoft's dominance in the computer industry than by an interest in furthering technology.

In these books, young readers will encounter inspiring stories about real people who achieved success despite enormous obstacles. Oprah Winfrey—the most powerful, most watched, and wealthiest woman on television today—spent the first six years of her life in the care of her grandparents while her unwed mother sought work and a better life elsewhere. Her adolescence was colored by promiscuity, pregnancy at age fourteen, rape, and sexual abuse.

Each author documents and supports his or her work with an array of primary and secondary source quotations taken from diaries, letters, speeches, and interviews. All quotes are footnoted to show readers exactly how and where biographers derive their information and provide guidance for further research. The quotations enliven the text by giving readers eyewitness views of the life and accomplishments of each person covered in the People in the News series.

In addition, each book in the series includes photographs, annotated bibliographies, timelines, and comprehensive indexes. For both the casual reader and the student researcher, the People in the News series offers insight into the lives of today's newsmakers—people who shape the way we live, work, and play in the modern age.

A Star on Many Levels

Will Smith is a star in the entertainment business. But asking three different people what he is famous for could draw three different answers. One person might rave about his skill at writing rap music. Another would likely remember Smith's popular television show *The Fresh Prince of Bel-Air*. Still another might praise Smith for his roles in blockbuster movies. He has proven himself to be a capable performer in all these areas and more.

Before he finished high school, Smith was entertaining audiences as a rap singer and songwriter under the stage name Fresh Prince. From his first hit single, "Girls Ain't Nothing But Trouble," in 1986 to his album *Willennium,* released in 1999, he has remained popular with rap music fans. His music has been used on the soundtracks of some of his movies—which have been just as successful as the films themselves. His records have gone platinum, and he has an impressive list of awards for excellence in music, including four Grammys.

The videos of Smith's rap music broadcast on MTV encouraged entertainment mogul Quincy Jones and studio executive Benny Medina to cast Smith as the main character in a television comedy series, *The Fresh Prince of Bel-Air,* which was the powerhouse of NBC's lineup until 1996, when Smith fulfilled his contract and left to pursue a career on the big screen.

Even before his television show was declared a hit, Smith was preparing himself for movie stardom. His ambitious plan was to make a name for himself with small roles in low-profile movies while he developed his acting skills, then move on to bigger roles in bigger-budget movies until he was as sought after by directors as superstars Tom Hanks and Tom Cruise. In later years, he has refined his goal to include recognition as the most versatile actor in Hollywood.

Accomplishing His Goals

Smith, at age thirty-four, is well on his way to accomplishing both goals. His two back-to-back blockbusters *Independence Day* and *Men in Black* made him one of the elite circle of leading men who are the first or second choice of casting departments for

Will Smith poses with his wife Jada and son Trey at the Golden Globe Awards. Smith is one of the most successful entertainers in show business.

plum roles. His widely varied past roles have included such diverse characters as a homosexual con man, a black government agent in a cowboy outfit, a mystical golf expert, and a champion boxer. To each role he has brought intelligence and dedication.

A Family Man

Smith is equally dedicated to his family. His parents taught him the value of an education and of hard work. They gave him confidence in himself and a strong sense of integrity. From them he learned that family is more important than money.

Although Smith has taken personal relationships seriously, his first marriage ended in divorce. In the aftermath of that failure, he has managed to remain active in his son Trey's life and to find happiness with his second wife, Jada Pinkett Smith. Will and Jada seem deeply committed to each other and to responsibly raising their three children.

A Model African American

Smith's personal and professional example has made him a model for black Americans. His charm and sense of humor come through in his rap music, his television show, and his movies. His appeal crosses racial lines, and his success in roles cast without regard to race has opened new doors for other black actors.

Will Smith, actor and rap star, is a man universally liked and greatly admired. He is a man worth getting to know.

A Solid Base to Jump From

Willard C. Smith II was born on September 25, 1968. His parents had high hopes for their son; as African Americans during the civil rights movement of the 1960s, Willard C. Smith Sr. and his wife, Carolyn, were eager to raise children who could take advantage of the new opportunities Martin Luther King Jr. and other black leaders had won for them.

Willard II's parents believed that the keys to success were a good education, strong self-discipline, a healthy work ethic, and above all, self-confidence, so these were the traits they tried to instill in their son. The Smiths had no theatrical ambitions for Will, yet the values they taught prepared him well for life in the spotlight.

Will Smith is aware of the debt he owes to his parents and is quick to give them credit. He says, "There are individual personality traits of celebrities and sports stars and people whom I admire, but the only people I ever idolized are my parents."[1]

Will's Father

Will's family lived in Wynnefield, Pennsylvania, a middle-class suburb of West Philadelphia. The family included two sisters, Pam and Ellen, and one brother, Harry. His two grandmothers, two great-grandmothers, and one great-great-grandmother also had a hand in shaping Will's character.

The senior Smith owned a business that set up refrigeration units in supermarkets. Although the business was successful, money was often tight. Will did not get everything he wanted,

Will Smith grew up in a world of opportunity and possibility, thanks in large part to the efforts of Dr. Martin Luther King Jr. (pictured) during the black civil rights movement of the 1960s.

but he always felt secure. If he had understood the family's finances better at the time, however, Will might have been uneasy. He told *Rolling Stone* in December 1998, "We were more broke than we thought we were because my father always had cash—that's how people paid him. But, often, all the cash he had was all the money the family had."[2]

Will's father had once served in the U.S. Air Force, and he continued to stress discipline at home, including physical punishment. However, Smith was also fair. Will told David Ritz of *Essence* magazine: "Dad was tough but not tyrannical. He'd get this look that said, 'One more step, Will, and it'll get ugly.'"[3] Will knew that if he ignored his father he was in for a spanking.

Besides making sure his children stayed out of trouble, Willard Sr. taught his sons to finish any job they undertook. One particular lesson made a deep impression on Will. When he was about fifteen years old, Will's father insisted that his two sons demolish and rebuild a decaying brick wall. For nearly six months the boys worked on the wall, even mixing the cement themselves. When they finally finished the job, they were immensely proud of themselves. Will said, "Dad told me and my brother, 'Now don't you all ever tell me you can't do something.' I look back on that a lot of times in my life when I think I won't be able to do something, and I tell myself, 'One brick at a time.'"[4]

Besides assigning his sons jobs around the home, Will's father expected them to help with refrigeration projects. On those service calls, Will learned additional lessons about doing a job right in spite of obstacles. He tells the following story:

> Now my father, he was a man who could do some work. We would do installations, put these big freezer cases in supermarkets. A lot of times we ended up working in the basement. A supermarket basement is the nastiest place that you could ever be in your life.
>
> One time we were in this place, and there was like two inches of muddy thick old food gunk on the floor, and there was a big old dead rat. My father, with his bare hands, picked up the rat and threw it out of the way. Then he put his head down on the floor right where the dead rat had been and went to work.
>
> What I do is difficult sometimes. What my father did was real hard work. I thank God every day that I don't have to feed my family by shoving rats out of the way.[5]

As an adult, Will is thankful for the lessons he learned. But when he was a teenager, his father's demands seemed to get in the way of his social life. One morning, when he had gotten home only a few hours before his father expected him on the job, Will was holding a flashlight so that his father could see the electrical wires inside a refrigeration unit. He fell asleep and awoke to cries of pain from his father who had touched the wrong wire because of the unsteady flashlight. Will realized that his father could have been killed because of his carelessness. That experience taught Will the importance of focusing on the job at hand. Later he often quoted his father's favorite slogan:

"Make sure you can focus. If you do one thing well, everything else will come from that."[6]

Will's Mother

Will's mother agreed with that philosophy, and she believed that her son's main focus should be on getting an education. She worked as a school secretary and wanted her children to have every chance to excel as students. Since Our Lady of Lourdes, a mostly white private Catholic school, was considered the best in the area, that is where Will went from kindergarten through eighth grade. Mrs. Smith insisted on enrolling Will there even though it taxed the family budget, the school was a forty-five-minute drive from home, and the Smiths were Baptists.

Although Will enjoyed going to Our Lady of Lourdes, he also found racism there. He told a reporter: "One of the nuns called me a nigger. I couldn't believe it. I was like, Wow, how did God put her in charge? At that point in my life, I had been called a nigger enough times that the word didn't hurt. It was just the shock that it came from a nun."[7]

This incident was not typical, however, and Will did well in grade school, especially in math, science, and English. He was not an enthusiastic reader, but he loved to make up poems and stories in which he was saving the world. He also liked to read Dr. Seuss books, with rhyming wordplay that he points out is a lot like the lyrics in rap music.

And Will learned other lessons beyond the basic school curriculum. His mother was an excellent pianist who taught him some of the fundamentals of playing the piano. All the Smiths played some kind of instrument, and Will would sit in on drums when his family played together for their own entertainment. He was for a time a member of his school band.

Will's mother also exposed her children to travel. When he was about seven, the family went to Yellowstone National Park, Mount Rushmore, the Alamo, and the Grand Canyon. Will said later that this cross-country trip helped him to understand the world more clearly.

But a well-rounded education was not all that Mrs. Smith emphasized. She taught Will to respect his elders, particularly women. He tells a story about when he was first learning to drive and his mother had agreed to ride with him. In his excitement about driving, Will raced around the car and jumped into the driver's seat and waited. But his mother did not get in. Finally, Will realized she wasn't going anywhere until he opened the door for her. Mrs. Smith expected a lot from Will, but he knew he could always count on her when things got rough.

The Rest of the Family

Will knew that his older sister Pam would back him up, too. When he was about nine years old, some older kids pulled a knife on him and stole his money. Will came home crying, and Pam, who was about fifteen then, literally went to bat for him. Will told *Rolling Stone,* "My older sister grabbed a bat and we walked around the neighborhood. I remember thinking . . . 'This is the person you want in your corner.' My older sister made me feel safe."[8]

Smith has always used his lively sense of humor to make people laugh. Here, he playfully palms the bald head of rap mogul Russell Simmons at the Source Hip Hop Awards.

His younger sister and brother, twins Ellen and Harry, were more inclined to bring out the mischief in Will. When all three of them faced spankings from their father, Will took the punishment in stride. Brother Harry, who is now Will's accountant, remembers: "Will was punished first because he's older. Then he'd go around a corner and make faces so we'd laugh—and we'd get punished worse." Ellen adds, "Will did the gross things kids do, like put straws up his nose."[9]

Will was always funny, and at the supper table he joined the family competition to get the biggest laugh. It was the perfect training ground for Will to hone his quick wit and clever delivery for the future. When Will's grandmother Helen Bright saw how much he loved being the center of attention, she cast him in little dramas she organized at their church. From those experiences he learned how to deliver a line, how to work an audience, and how to effectively use language.

Using correct English was important at the Smith home, and profanity was not allowed. Will, however, was constantly around other teens who swore casually, and he acquired a habit of tough talk to fit in with his peers. At age eleven he discovered rap music. After that all he wanted to do was write rap lyrics. He copied the songs he heard with his friends, which usually included profanity and tales of sexual conquest.

Will thought he could use such words in his own rhymes, but his grandmother soon set him straight. Will says when his grandmother happened to see what was in his rap book, she wrote a little note on one of the pages. It said, "Dear Will, Truly intelligent people do not have to use this type of language to express themselves. Why don't you show the world that you are as smart as we all think you are?"[10] From then on Will kept his rap lyrics clean.

Overbrook High School

Will was already rapping up a storm when he transferred in ninth grade to public Overbrook High School, which helped offset some of the culture shock associated with the move. After having gone to an almost all white school, Will's rap music helped him to fit in at the mostly black Overbrook. Will later suggested

Smith's senior year photo from Overbrook High School, where he felt at home among the predominantly black student body.

his experience in different school environments and a mixed-culture home neighborhood, which included Jews and Muslims, was one of the keys to his success. He said, "I have a great understanding of what black people think is funny and what white people think is funny. I'm able to find the joke that everyone thinks is hilarious."[11] In addition, Will learned to be comfortable among different races and to put others at ease around him.

Will's sense of humor made him popular with most of the students at Overbrook, but sometimes he got teased about his big ears. One guy in particular told Will that he looked like a car with both doors open. Even after he had become a big star, Will was still a little self-conscious about his ears. When a writer from *Ebony* asked Will why he thought Americans loved him so much, Will said, "It's the ears! Americans have an ear fetish. Absolutely. Americans love people with big ears—Mickey Mouse, Goofy, Ross Perot. Americans love ears."[12]

Will's success as class clown did not help him academically, but he devised a strategy for getting by without doing homework.

He told reporter Michael Fleming that after being told home-work would be 10 percent of his grade, "I decided I'd get *A*'s on all my tests. . . . If I got *A*'s everywhere else, I'd get 90 percent. If I got *B*'s, that's an 80 percent, and still a *B*. My mother hated that I would let my mind go to all that trouble to figure out how to get a *B*."[13]

Will knew his teachers would not accept deliberate neglect of schoolwork, so he invented clever excuses for being unpre-pared that he delivered with great charm. Some of the teachers were amused, and they took to calling him Prince Charming. Will didn't mind this nickname, but he put the word *fresh* in front of "Prince" and dropped the "Charming," because in Philadel-phia slang *fresh* meant "new" or "very good."

The Roots of Rap Music

Rap music emerged in poor areas of the Bronx (in New York City) in the early 1990s, and it was part of a new subculture known as hip-hop. This was a culture born of necessity. Kids who wanted to dance had no place to perform, so they carried around pieces of cardboard, which they used for dancing on the sidewalk. Kids with poetry in their souls scrawled graffiti on subway entrances, and rappers pur-ported to tell gritty personal stories in rhyming wordplay set to the music they listened to. Because the hardships of ghetto life made these teens angry and frustrated, these personal stories were often laced with profanity and violent imagery.

In those early days DJs, who played seven-inch, 45-rpm records at neighborhood dance parties, gave out calls to get the dancers fired up. Usually these calls were given during breaks in the vocal part of the record, somewhat like a jazz drummer adding a few licks between lines of a song. Break dancers also used these breaks to put on a show.

Gradually the kids became more interested in the breaks than in the music itself. To make the breaks last longer, DJs began using two turntables and switching back and forth from the break on one record to the break on the other. Records were purposely "scratched" to help the DJ find the correct spot. This technique of putting together bits of background music to make the breaks last longer became an art form of its own. When DJs got too busy to make their own calls, they let other kids take over the microphones. These kids came up with longer and more complicated rhythmic rhymes, and the callers came to be referred to as rappers.

Other Influences

Although the Fresh Prince lacked enthusiasm for homework, he had plenty of enthusiasm for sports, movies, and television shows. He especially loved basketball, and his favorite player was hometown hero Julius Erving. In the entertainment field, he idolized Eddie Murphy. Will spent a lot of time standing in front of mirrors at his house trying his best to look and sound like the comedian. Will also looked up to Philadelphia natives Bill Cosby and astronaut Guion Bluford. This group of men had gained new respect for blacks, and Will dreamed of following their lead.

With such fine role models and parents, Will was never interested in trying drugs. But his father wanted to be sure that his son would continue to shun them, so one day he took Will for a ride. They went through one of the worst areas of Philadelphia and Will's father told him to look at the bums sleeping in the streets. Then his father said, "This is what people look like when they do drugs."[14] Will always remembered that lesson.

Likewise, he saw smoking as a disgusting habit. Will says, "Smoking is just totally unbearable. The whole idea is nasty. . . . I like to kiss, and just can't kiss someone who is all smoked out."[15]

The Divorce

Will's parents had formed a strong alliance to prepare him for responsible adulthood, but when he reached thirteen, their partnership failed and the Smiths divorced. The divorce could have been difficult for Will, but fortunately it didn't turn out that way. Will was relieved by the end of his parents' bickering and the constant tension in the house, and his own circumstances underwent no drastic change. His mother simply took Will and his siblings to another part of the neighborhood to live with his grandmother. Will's father continued to be involved in Will's life, and both parents worked hard to make sure the children still felt safe and loved.

He sums up life after the divorce like this:

> We never felt like our parents didn't love us. No matter how difficult things got or how angry someone may have gotten, no matter what happened in our lives, we always

Will Smith and Basketball

Smith has loved the game of basketball since childhood. In high school, two of his biggest heroes were basketball stars Wilt Chamberlain and Julius Erving. Julius Erving, known as Doctor J, played for Smith's home team the Philadelphia '76ers and made an especially big impression.

Later in life when people questioned Smith about where he got the courage to face the greatest challenges in his career, he would say he was following Erving's example. He said that, like Dr. J, no matter how tough the situation he faced, he would always take the shot.

Julius Erving, one of the adolescent Smith's biggest heroes, returns to earth after dunking the ball.

felt that we had somewhere to go. You can't spring off into the world from a flimsy base. You've got to have a solid base to jump from.[16]

Will's parents gave him such a base. In the years that followed he used all their gifts to become not only one of the most successful black entertainers but one of the world's most popular and versatile stars of any color.

Chapter 2

The Fresh Prince of Philadelphia

It didn't take Will Smith long to use the skills and attitudes his parents had instilled in him to find success. His ability to tell funny stories, his love of music, and his urge to get ahead enabled him to break into the rap music business, and success followed quickly.

From Will's first hearing in 1979 of "Rapper's Delight," the first rap record marketed to the general public, he was hooked. On this record, three black men took turns boasting and poking fun at each other over a background of rhythm and harmonies that had been borrowed (or "sampled") from an earlier hit tune called "Good Times." The effect was like listening in at a party, and it reached an audience, black and white, outside the urban black community where rap originated.

The pioneers of rap music, however, thought "Rapper's Delight" was just plain dumb. According to rapper Melle Mel, "We laughed when we first heard it. The group was called the Sugar Hill Gang, and they weren't even from the Bronx. Every rapper hated it."[17] Russell Simmons, who would soon establish Def Jam Records to specialize in rap music, remembers this record left him feeling distraught, and he was angry about what this group of imposters had stolen from the rap community.

Later, however, Simmons changed his mind. In an interview on National Public Radio, he said he finally realized this record was actually "the greatest thing that could have happened,"[18] because "Rapper's Delight" made rap music appealing to people of all races. It tapped into a huge audience that he and future rappers, such as Will Smith, made a fortune from.

Russell Simmons (pictured) established Def Jam Records at a time when rap was struggling to define itself as a musical genre.

Just for Fun

But neither Will nor his parents were thinking about rap music in terms of making money back in 1979. They just figured it would be a nice hobby and his parents happily bought Will the equipment he said he needed. His first goal was to become a DJ—short for disc jockey—and to control the "wheels of steel," rappers' slang for the dual record turntables that helped produce the distinctive rap sound.

In hindsight it might seem that Smith's skill with words and ability to make people laugh would have drawn him to perform as a rapper rather than a DJ. But twelve-year-old Will focused on playing the music, and spent countless hours in his basement experimenting with the turntables. He was good at it, and eventually was asked to perform as a DJ at local parties and church functions.

But being just good was not good enough for Smith, and he finally realized that he would never be the best DJ around. From then on Will dedicated himself to writing rap lyrics. He says, "I started rapping just as soon as I heard that first song. I rapped all day long, until I thought my mom was going to lose her mind! Music, after all, has always been in my heart. At first I did it as a hobby and I enjoyed it and I got really good at it."[19] In fact, Will soon became the star of local "shoot-outs," group rap sessions in which each rapper tried to get the best response from the crowd with his extemporaneous lyrics. Even today Smith brags that he never lost a street battle.

First Partner

Rappers and DJs worked as teams in shoot-outs, so they looked for partners whose styles complemented their own. Will's first partner was a friend named Clarence "Kate" Holmes who called himself Ready Rock-C. Will, using his alias Fresh Prince, provided the lyrics, and together he and Kate established a reputation in Philadelphia for their humor.

When Will was fourteen, the boys, confident that they could cut a successful record, approached Dana Goodman, who ran a small recording company called Word Up. Goodman said they showed promise but told them to write more songs before they approached him again.

So the duo wrote more songs, and they were invited to perform at so many parties that they began to charge for their services. Will was having a great time and making a few bucks, and that was enough for the time being.

Hooking Up with Jeff Townes

Then, early in 1986, Smith met Jeff Townes, an older boy in the community, who was already a minor celebrity in their part of Philadelphia as Jazzy Jeff. The nickname came from Townes's habit of sampling serious jazz recordings for his backgrounds rather than cuts by R&B stars like James Brown and George Clinton who were popular among other DJs.

Townes was going to DJ at a party in Smith's neighborhood, so Smith went to hear him. Smith listened for a while, then asked to do a rap or two with Townes's group. Both Townes and Smith immediately felt there was a special chemistry between them.

Townes told a reporter from *People,* "I'd worked with 2000 crews before I found this maniac. There was a click when I worked with him that was missing before."[20] Townes says he dreamed about Smith that night and called him up the next day. For a while Townes and Smith and Holmes worked as a three-some, often around Smith's kitchen table drinking Kool-Aid.

In 1986, before Smith's senior year in high school, the boys went back to Dana Goodman, and he offered them a one-shot record contract. Their debut single, "Girls Ain't Nothing But Trouble," was the lament of a boy who has had trouble with girls and wants to warn others about the opposite sex. It was a humorous story that teenagers could relate to.

Then Smith, still a teen himself, had to get back to school. It was his final year before college, and his mother had plans for

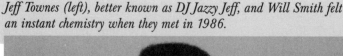

Jeff Townes (left), better known as DJ Jazzy Jeff, and Will Smith felt an instant chemistry when they met in 1986.

his future. She was hoping that he would win a scholarship and study to become a computer engineer.

Record Is a Hit

But before Smith could finish high school, his first record was released, and his life got complicated. Suddenly "Girls Ain't Nothing But Trouble" was getting heavy air time on the rap and R&B stations of Philadelphia, and Smith began to have second thoughts about college. A representative from Jive Records wanted to sign the boys to a contract and give their hit single national exposure. Soon "Girls Ain't Nothing But Trouble" was popular all over the United States and in many foreign countries. It sold more than one hundred thousand copies.

Compared with that kind of excitement, even the scholarship Smith was offered by Massachusetts Institute of Technology (MIT) failed to impress him. When his mother insisted he at least visit MIT's campus, her plan backfired. Smith told *Rolling Stone*, "I was scared of it. It just looked hard. She couldn't believe I'd give up MIT for rap."[21]

Smith's father wished he would go to college, too, but Willard Sr. said, "Let him do what he wants. He's not going to be happy if he doesn't make his own decisions about life."[22] So, Willard II skipped college to seek his fortune elsewhere.

And that fortune was just over the horizon. Soon the money started coming in, and Smith and Townes toured the British Isles with rap legends like LL Cool J and Public Enemy. When they arrived in London, they were mobbed by fans—giving their egos an even bigger boost.

Smith said, "There were screaming girls at the airport, and we just thought, 'What is this? What are they screaming for?'"[23] They soon learned that "Girls Ain't Nothing But Trouble" was a bigger hit in England than it was in the United States.

Criticism

The record was a hit across gender and color lines. Even Smith's mother approved of it, but just as "Rapper's Delight" had done earlier, Smith and Townes's party music offended hardcore rappers. People like Big Daddy Kane complained that because

Will Defends "Girls Ain't Nothing But Trouble"

In addition to the criticism that Smith and Townes took from hardcore rappers over their first single—which also was included on the album *Rock the House*—for being too middle class, they received complaints from feminists for supposedly insulting women. Will defended the record by saying that his lyrics weren't intended as a statement of fact, only as one person's view about what had happened to him.

He gave the feminists a nod on his second album, *He's the DJ, I'm the Rapper*. It included a duet he did with a female rapper on a song called "Guys Ain't Nothing But Trouble," which supposedly gave women equal time.

Smith and Townes were from the suburbs, their music didn't really qualify as rap.

Smith insisted his music was just as much about the black experience as anyone else's. He told Jeff Ressner of *Rolling Stone:* "Our music is black music. Our families are black; we come from black backgrounds."[24] He went on to suggest that Big Daddy Kane's real problem with Smith's lyrics was that they were intelligent. Smith said, "Somewhere along the line it became cool to be ignorant. I don't understand that. I don't understand how people can think it's cool not to be articulate. He [Big Daddy Kane] thinks being articulate is being white."[25]

First Albums

Despite the criticism, Smith and Townes wrote more rap music for Jive Records and put together an album they called *Rock the House*. The title cut was by Kate Holmes and "Girls Ain't Nothing But Trouble" was on it, too. The album sold more than six hundred thousand copies.

Jazzy Jeff and the Fresh Prince needed a follow-up album fast to take advantage of their momentum. Jive Records said that the boys could do whatever they wanted, so they put together the first double hip-hop album in music history. *He's the DJ, I'm the Rapper* was released in 1988.

This album was an even bigger hit than *Rock the House,* with sales fueled by two enormously popular singles. On the funny "Parents Just Don't Understand," Smith pretends to be a boy whose mother wants to buy him a school wardrobe that is hopelessly out-of-date. He claims his mom just doesn't understand. Smith's video of this single ran regularly on MTV and boosted record sales. Another cut, "Nightmare on My Street," was a takeoff on "Nightmare on Elm Street" and other horror movies. To Smith's delight, the album sold over 3 million copies.

Reckless Spending

At this point money was simply pouring into Smith's bank account, and he began to think he could never spend it all. He spent recklessly, buying expensive clothes, jewelry, and a mansion in the suburbs. He took fifteen of his childhood buddies along on tour and on vacations. He bought six cars (including a Corvette, Camaro, and Suburban) and a Suzuki motorbike. His parents were disgusted with him. His father said, "What do you need six cars for when you only have one butt?"[26] In 1988 Smith estimates that he spent about $800,000.

Racial Encounters

But sudden wealth didn't mean that Smith was immune from racism. Before his success as a rapper, he had been harassed by police officers who pulled him over just because he was driving a nice car. He remembers one such incident in particular. When Smith asked, "Officer, did I do something?" The policeman said, "You're a —— nigger in a nice car. Now shut the —— up until I figure out why I'm giving you a ticket."[27]

When Smith began driving luxury cars, such incidents became almost routine. Smith had said, "In the two years I've had my Corvette, I probably got stopped thirty-five or forty times. At least five to ten of those times, I was told I was stopped because, 'We want to know where you got this car.' A young black guy with a nice car is going to get stopped, period. And the cops will tell you that."[28] When he sat in the first-class section in airplanes, Smith was also likely to be challenged about whether or not he belonged there.

But in spite of the racism he encountered in real life, Americans of all colors were finding they liked Smith's rap lyrics and could relate to them. Because Smith's stories were humorous rather than violent, he and Townes were invited to play in places that shunned hardcore rappers. DJ Jazzy Jeff and the Fresh Prince started to receive awards for their work, too. At the 1989 American Music Awards *He's the DJ, I'm the Rapper* won Best Rap Album, and "Parents Just Don't Understand" was named Best Rap Single. Then they learned that the Grammy Awards committee had decided to add rap music to its award categories for the first time, and that "Parents Just Don't Understand" was one of the nominees for Best Song.

Smith and Townes were thrilled by the prospect of appearing on national television to accept one of the coveted statues. But then they heard the rest of the story. Rap was still perceived as music from the black ghetto subculture and given little status, so the award was to be handed out at a prebroadcast ceremony whose winners would be announced as a group early in the evening of the televised ceremony. Smith and Townes and other rappers were so insulted they decided to boycott the whole affair, and their stand got results. The following year the rap music awards were given during the broadcast with other premier performance categories.

Personal Problems

With all the money and awards he was earning, Smith should have been on top of the world, and in many ways he was. But his personal life was not going as well. Smith had been in love with a high school sweetheart since he was fifteen, and he had been faithful to her, avoiding backstage groupies and casual flings. But when Smith was eighteen, he was devastated to learn

A Smart Business Move

Early in their career, Smith and his partner Jeff Townes thought of a clever way to make an enormous amount of money in addition to what they were raking in on record sales and personal appearances. They started their own "900" phone line where kids could pay to call in and get the latest information about the rap duo. The phone line was so popular that it had more than 2 million calls in the first six months.

DJ Jazzy Jeff (left) and the Fresh Prince (right) were an extremely successful rap duo, but the excesses of celebrity led the pair to the brink of bankruptcy.

that this special girl had cheated on him. In an interview he gave twelve years later, he told Nancy Collins of *Rolling Stone:* "The most emotional pain I [have] ever felt was when my first girl-friend cheated on me. That was like a complete destruction of what I thought the world was. It was the first and biggest thing that ever happened—a 9.0 on the Richter scale."[29] The relation-ship soon ended, and Smith admits that after that he went a little wild with women. A few months of playing the field, how-ever, left him feeling more empty than ever.

The End of the Poetry

When Jive Records asked the boys to make a third album, Smith and Townes decided that the Bahamas would be a nice place to work. They rented a mansion near the beach and took all their friends along for the party. This was a mistake: Almost no work got done in such an atmosphere, and Smith and Townes had to come home to finish their album *And in This Corner.*

And the Internal Revenue Service arrived soon after that to point out an even bigger mistake. Smith hadn't bothered to hire an accountant or a business manager to handle his finances and he had assumed taxes were already taken out of the huge checks he was receiving. He had assumed wrong, and the U.S. government slapped him with a tax bill of several million dollars. That was a lot more money than he had left, and Smith had no idea how he was going to pay.

Suddenly Smith was not only broke but deeply in debt. He said later, "There's nothing more sobering than having six cars and a mansion one day and you can't even buy gas for the cars the next."[30] The party was clearly over, and he needed to make a lot of money in a hurry.

At first he hoped that his new album might bail him out. But when *And in This Corner* came out in 1989, it was soon obvious that it would not be as successful as *He's the DJ, I'm the Rapper* had been. Although it sold over a million copies, it would not give Smith the kind of money he needed to pay off Uncle Sam. He took small comfort from the fact that the single "I Think I Can Beat Mike Tyson" from the album was a hit and brought in another Grammy nomination. Smith needed a way to earn a great deal of money, something that paid better than rap music. And he thought he knew the way.

Chapter 3

The Fresh Prince of Bel-Air

Smith had earned and lost a fortune by the time he reached his twentieth birthday. In fact, by 1989, he was so deeply in debt that he needed to make another fortune just to pay his back taxes. His parents had taught him to always learn from his mistakes and move on, so Smith did just that. He sold his mansion and his cars and began to consider his options. Acting had always appealed to him, and he figured that Hollywood stars make more money than rappers. Maybe he would try to become an actor.

Of course, Smith realized that only a tiny percentage of the wanna-bes who flock to Hollywood actually get cast in movies, much less make any money. But his videos had been so popular on MTV that several big names in the entertainment business had already suggested that Smith might have a future in front of the cameras. When he and Townes were invited to perform at Disneyland in late 1989, the time seemed right for Smith to try his luck.

And the possibility of a new career wasn't the only reason Smith wanted to spend time in the Los Angeles area. His ulterior motive was named Tanya Moore. Smith had spotted this beautiful coed in the audience the previous year when he was performing at San Diego State University. They had dated whenever possible ever since, and now Moore had a job and an apartment in Los Angeles. It was a place Smith could use as home base while he looked for work.

Smith and Townes finished work at Disneyland, and Townes flew back to Philadelphia while Smith moved in with Moore. Then Smith started making the rounds of the studios to let everyone know he was available. He got nowhere at first, but one day he was hanging around backstage at the Arsenio Hall Show when the special guest was the gifted, one-man entertainment business Quincy Jones. A young vice president from Warner Brothers, Benny Medina, who was a close friend of Jones's, was there, too, and he recognized Smith from his rap music. The two began talking. Smith told Medina that he wanted to become an actor. Medina told Smith about a new television show he planned to offer NBC that was based on his own life story.

Medina's early years had been in Watts, a tough part of East Los Angeles. When his mother died and his father abandoned him, he was shuffled from one foster home to another. His future looked grim until a wealthy white bandleader named Jack Elliott took him in. Medina had faced serious culture shock at first, but eventually he became president of his class and a star in both football and drama. He thought this situation could be the basis for a comedy series, but that the story might be more interesting if the rich family was black instead of white.

Pitching the Idea

Medina was almost ready to pitch his idea to NBC, and he decided Smith was the perfect person to play the main character. Smith was interested, so Medina said that he would talk to Jones about it. Jones liked Medina's idea and commented that he knew NBC was looking for a comedy to replace *Alf* on Monday nights. He thought NBC would be interested in a show that would appeal to largely untapped audiences of blacks and teens. In other words, he thought Medina's idea was one whose time had come.

The next step was to get an audience with Brandon Tartikoff, head of NBC Entertainment. It took a month to set up an eight-minute interview. When he finally got his chance, Medina talked as fast as he could, but suddenly Tartikoff got up, headed for the door, and mumbled, "cute life."[31] Both Medina and Jones figured they had struck out. But the next day Tartikoff's office called Medina with an offer to do the show. They would also consider Smith for the leading role, but he would need to audition. Medina agreed that was only good business.

Producer and composer Quincy Jones (here conducting a rehearsal) played a pivotal role in launching Will Smith's television career.

Then NBC dropped the bombshell. Smith's audition was scheduled for that very night. Medina, who wasn't even sure how to find Smith, said that was impossible. All he knew was that Smith and Townes were on a concert tour somewhere out East. But the NBC representative said, "Now or never,"[32] so Medina agreed to try.

The Audition

Smith was in Indianapolis when he got the call, and he was on the next plane west. By 10:15 P.M. he was at Quincy Jones's mansion in Bel Air with a group of executives from NBC. Smith was given a script and sent into a spare bedroom to read it through. The pressure was on.

Smith was nervous, but determined to do his best. He said later, "I wasn't scared because I knew this was what I had to do. I had scheduled readings for *Cosby* and *Different World*, but I didn't go to them. I was scared. I was making excuses. But when this came up I said to myself: 'This is my shot. I'm taking whatever happens.'"[33]

What happened was good. When Smith finished reading, NBC couldn't sign him fast enough. Warren Littlefield, NBC's entertainment president at the time, recalls it this way, "Will read from a script and nailed it. I sat there thinking, 'Whoa! Just bottle this guy!'"[34] Medina told *Ebony* he remembered that shortly after that the NBC executives were out in front of Jones's home calling each other from their limos and signing the paperwork.

Smith was thrilled to suddenly have his own weekly television show. Now he would have a way to pay his back taxes. Indeed, the IRS planned to take 72 percent of everything he made; if the show was a success, Smith would be out from under his debts in three years.

The Challenge

But there was no guarantee—network critics were predicting the show would be a disaster and expressing serious doubts that an untrained newcomer, who had never acted except in his grandmother's church plays, could carry a big-time television series. Furthermore, the show was going to be about young black people and rap music. Since most adults associated that sort of music with violence and ghetto culture, analysts assumed the show would not appeal to the general public.

But Will Smith was charming, full of self-confidence, and quick to catch on in new situations. Also, many things about the show worked in his favor. His character on the program was a younger version of himself, by about four years. In fact, the main character was a rapper from Philadelphia whose name was Will Smith. Instead of downplaying the rap connection, NBC decided to exploit it and dubbed the show *The Fresh Prince of Bel-Air.*

Although the real Fresh Prince didn't move to Bel Air, he did move to Burbank so that he could be near the soundstage where his show would be filmed. He rented an apartment there and Moore moved in with him. Then he went to work. Smith wrote a rap song that would become the show's theme and gave the show's team of white writers a crash course in hip-hop and black culture.

Will and Tatyana

When Smith first started doing his TV show, Tatyana Ali, who played his little sister, had nothing but scorn for his acting, even though she thought his rap music was great. But gradually she learned to like him and to respect the way he treated the other people on the show. She said that he was always giving everyone a big hug in the morning and leading pep sessions.

On one episode of *The Fresh Prince of Bel-Air*, Tatyana had the chance to sing an Aretha Franklin tune. Smith was quick to compliment her on her singing and encouraged her to do more in the future. In 1998, he signed Tatyana to sing for his production company Will Smith Enterprises and shepherded her through the process of making her first single, "Daydreamin.'"

Will Smith (rear) encouraged Tatyana Ali (center) to pursue a singing career.

With Smith's help, the writers struggled to write a pilot episode. Meanwhile, the show's cast was gradually assembled. James Avery was hired to play Smith's uncle, a lawyer named Philip Banks, and Janet Hubert-Whitten was cast as his Aunt Viv. The rest of the cast included Alfonso Ribeiro as Cousin Carlton, Karyn Parson as Cousin Hilary, Tatyana Ali as little Cousin Ashley, and Joseph Marcell as the butler. All had lengthy acting resumes, yet they were soon to serve as supporting characters assigned to make a complete rookie look good. Not surprisingly, there were problems ahead.

Rookie Actor

When Smith saw how professional the other actors on his show were and realized the position he had gotten himself into, he got a little scared. He didn't want to look like an amateur, so he worked hard to prepare himself for his first day on the set. He spent hours learning the entire script, only to see his hard work backfire.

As Smith told a reporter in a 2001 interview:

> I learned from my father that a huge part of success is a willingness to work so I made it a point to learn every single word of dialogue in the script. While I waited my

The cast of The Fresh Prince *poses on the set of the show. With no acting experience, Smith (seated) found it challenging to work alongside his more practiced colleagues.*

turn, I'd mouth everyone else's lines. It took about six episodes for somebody to notice and say something [like "Stop it"] because you tend to look at who's talking.[35]

And the untrained Smith had other problems to overcome. At first he said his lines in a normal speaking voice, and it was hard to understand what he was saying. He had to learn to project. Many times he was in the wrong place on the stage, so he had to learn to pay attention to the white marks that told him where the camera expected him to be. Smith was upset and embarrassed about his many mistakes, but NBC's executives told him he was doing fine.

When his writers were interviewed, they tried to sound positive about his acting, too. Andy Borowitz told *TV Guide* in 1990, "We're seeing an improvement every day. He [Smith] has a natural ability. It's not like we pulled some schmo off the street."[36]

The New Eddie Murphy

In spite of Smith's stumbles, a pilot episode was filmed and a test audience of young people was brought in to give their reactions to the show. To the producers' delight, *The Fresh Prince of Bel-Air* got the highest approval rating of any new comedy NBC had ever tested, and the NBC publicity machine shifted into high gear.

Tartikoff started referring to Smith as the new Eddie Murphy. He told *People* magazine, "Will has this very infectious personality, with a great spirit. Whatever he has, you can't teach. I think the Eddie Murphy comparison is there."[37] Smith was embarrassed by the hyperbole and said he felt like calling Murphy to apologize.

Then NBC reps started predicting that *The Fresh Prince of Bel-Air* would be a runaway hit. Again Smith was uneasy about all the bragging before the fact. He said, "Nobody knows what a runaway hit is until the fans say it's a runaway hit."[38]

The Rapster Is a Hit

Happily, in this case, the NBC reps turned out to be right. The new show debuted on September 10, 1990, and that first week it

A scene from The Fresh Prince. *The show helped discredit the stereotype that African Americans live in poverty in violent ghettos.*

won the ratings battle for its 7:00 P.M. time slot. Within a few weeks *The Fresh Prince* was crowned as the king of Monday night.

Having a hit TV show of his own was good for Smith, good for NBC, and good for black Americans. Too many rappers were stressing the violence and hopelessness that existed in black ghettos. *The Fresh Prince,* however, showed white America that African Americans often live in decent homes with stable families. Parents felt safe with Smith and his show while kids thought he was cool. In fact, a high school panel chosen by *TV Guide* gave *The Fresh Prince of Bel-Air* an "A- for coolness."[39]

Townes Comes West

As soon as *The Fresh Prince* was declared a hit, Smith used his new clout at NBC to get DJ Jazzy Jeff on the show. Again, the script mirrored real life in that Townes played Smith's best friend, a character they called Jazz. It was fun for Smith to have Townes to pal around with on the set, but more important, with

Townes in California, he and Smith could get to work on a new rap album. For Smith this meant working very long hours, but he did not mind. He said, "I'm doing the show from nine to five, and from six until midnight, I'm in the studio working on the album. As long as I get my eight hours of sleep, I'm fine."[40]

The new album was called *Homebase* and the boys cleverly premiered a song from the album, named "Summertime," on the television show. This helped the sales of both the single and the album go platinum. "Summertime" eventually won Smith and Townes a second Grammy award.

But bringing Townes on the show meant that the cast of *The Fresh Prince* was now working with two inexperienced actors. It was a situation that sometimes resulted in bickering and back-biting, and Smith took it upon himself to try to keep everyone happy. He was funny and mostly kind to his cast, and he enlivened the set with good-natured practical jokes. Once he even wrapped all the studio toilet seats in plastic wrap. He gave his TV family nice gifts, too, paying to redecorate their dressing rooms and taking them all to Hawaii. Eventually he won over most of his fellow cast members, and they worked well together.

Good-Bye Tanya, Hello Sheree

However, Smith and his girlfriend Tanya Moore had stopped working well together sometime during the first season of *The Fresh Prince*. It seemed that as his television career heated up, their relationship cooled. Moore began dating singing star Johnny Gill and Smith was left out. At first he took the breakup hard, but then he started pursuing a young fashion designer named Sheree Zampino, who finally agreed to go out with him after six months of Smith's pestering. He was his old cheerful self when he went off to film *Where the Day Takes You* in the summer of 1991, and he returned to *The Fresh Prince* that fall in great spirits.

In its second season, the show was an even bigger hit. It earned especially good reviews for its Christmas episode in which all the Banks family's Christmas gifts are stolen and the real importance of Christmas is examined. As Janet Hubert-Whitten put it, "You don't have to have material things. You give gifts from the heart."[41] Many people found this episode particularly touching and more realistic than the average *The Fresh Prince* show.

That Christmas Smith's personal life was especially warm as well. On Christmas Eve he proposed to Sheree and she accepted. They were married the following May. That summer Smith worked on a feature film, *Made in America,* before returning to get ready for the next season of *The Fresh Prince.*

In its third season the happy family that was seen every Monday night on television was under some stress. Janet Hubert-Whitten, who played Aunt Viv, and Smith were not getting along. Their arguments were increasingly open, and in 1993 Hubert-Whitten's contract was not renewed. She blamed Smith and took potshots at him in the media; Smith said she had a bad attitude on the set and claimed that she wanted to be the star of the show.

But the unpleasantness on the set during that third season didn't bother Smith too much, because he had more important

Smith smiles as he poses for the media with his wife, Sheree Zampino.

Will and Trey

Smith has said that the birth of his son Willard C. Smith III, whom he promptly dubbed "Trey," immediately caused him to see the world differently. Even the drive home from the hospital with this precious cargo was undertaken with caution. No more fast driving because Smith realized he was responsible for keeping the child safe.

Soon Trey was old enough to come on the set of *The Fresh Prince*, where he became a great favorite of the cast and crew. He was always well behaved and would shush everyone when he saw the red light come on indicating the cameras were rolling.

And Smith became a soccer dad, too, but sometimes at games he had a hard time keeping a straight face. As he told Nancy Collins of *Rolling Stone*, his son Trey had a habit of running full-out toward the ball only to pull back and let someone else kick it. Smith knew that Trey was capable of kicking the ball accurately because he had practiced with his son. Smith said,

> During time out, I call him to the sidelines. And he's winded, bent over with hands on his knees. So I say, "Trey, man, you been doing a great job, dude. But there's one little problem. You run really hard to the ball, but you're not kicking it." And he looks up at me and says, "What are you talking about? I'm all over the place out there." Back on the field I hear him saying, "I'm a machine. I'm a machine." And I'm crying. I try to discipline him, but he cracks me up. He's got so much personality.

Smith takes his son, Trey, by the hand. The birth of his son was a life-changing event for Will.

things on his mind. In December 1992 he became the father of Willard C. Smith III, and that spring he began preparing for a demanding role in a film to be called *Six Degrees of Separation*. It was the movie that would establish Smith as a serious actor rather than a TV star who dabbled in movie roles.

Chapter 4

Freshman Movie Actor

Smith's TV show *The Fresh Prince of Bel-Air* had done many good things for him. It had paid off his huge tax debt, made his face familiar to millions, and taught Smith how to handle himself in front of the cameras. But now his primary goal was to become a movie star, and he had already begun working toward that goal. Even though the odds were against him, his memories of a certain brick wall back in Philadelphia gave him self-confidence. In fact, he had begun to make plans for becoming a movie star soon after he arrived in Hollywood.

He told *Vibe*'s Mike Sager, "After I got the show, I said to my boys, 'Yo! Come on, full court press.' During those first three years of *The Fresh Prince,* we studied the entertainment business thoroughly. Every step we made was a calculated step."[42]

The Plan

Smith's plan was to make a movie each summer when *The Fresh Prince* went on hiatus. His first roles would be small parts in low-budget movies to avoid making a fool of himself while he learned how to act. Then he would move on to bigger, more challenging roles.

His 1991 project, *Where the Day Takes You,* fit the bill perfectly, and was a nice change of pace from his TV comedy. *Where the Day Takes You* was about a group of homeless kids living in Los Angeles. Smith's character, Manny, had to fend for himself as a homeless man while confined to a wheelchair. For Smith, playing a victim rather than a kid with a smart mouth was playing against type. In his biggest scene, Manny even got beaten up and tipped out of his wheelchair by thugs. This movie taught Smith not only about the process of filmmaking but also about the experience of being down and out.

He said, "Just seeing how people ignore the homeless was an amazing lesson. I was in full makeup on Hollywood Boulevard, and people didn't know me. It was a revelation in how cold people could be."[43] Although the film made little money, Smith was at least mentioned in some of the movie's reviews as having done a creditable job.

The Second Step

Smith applied for roles in several movies scheduled to be made during *The Fresh Prince*'s second hiatus, but none of those projects reached the film stage. Then he was cast as Tea Cake Walters, a supporting role in *Made in America,* starring Whoopi Goldberg and Ted Danson.

Smith's role was not challenging, but he set out to study the techniques of comedy stars of the big screen to capitalize on the

The cast of Made in America *in a movie still. Smith's supporting role was an important step in the development of his screen acting career.*

experience of working with seasoned professionals. He watched lots of movies starring Jim Carrey, Tom Hanks, Robin Williams, and Eddie Murphy, concluding, "Everything in movies is just a touch smaller, a touch slower, because the camera does more of the work."[44]

Armed with this knowledge he was ready to do his best in *Made in America,* an improbable comedy about a young black woman (the Walters character's girlfriend) who discovers that her father was a white sperm donor.

Being on the set with Danson and Goldberg was fun, but at one point Goldberg took it upon herself to discipline Smith. She made him see that shooting a movie was too expensive for him to clown around all the time as he did on the set of *The Fresh Prince.*

The movie was released in 1993 to mixed reviews. However, most critics had kind words for Smith. Rita Kempley of the *Washington Post* said, "Will Smith, TV's 'Fresh Prince of Bel-Air,' is riotous as her [Zora's] lovesick sidekick. Smith's shtick and probably his character are superfluous, but [director Richard] Benjamin sensibly indulges the young comic."[45] Getting more positive feedback for his work was nice, but Smith knew that he would have do something soon to make directors and producers stop seeing him as a silly teenager. He could not afford to be typecast if he hoped to be a big movie star.

The Big Step

Smith's next movie was exactly what his career needed, but personally it was a huge challenge. When he heard that a film called *Six Degrees of Separation* called for a young black man for an important role, he was immediately interested. The movie was to be an adaptation of an acclaimed, sophisticated Broadway stage play written by John Guare that had been a huge hit in London as well as New York. Guare's plot was based on a true incident in New York City in which a young black con artist succeeded in getting himself accepted as a houseguest by some of the wealthiest and most socially prominent people on Park Avenue by posing as Paul Poitier, son of actor Sidney Poitier.

Guare began with a fanciful theory that any two people in the world can be connected by six or fewer associations—each

A scene from Six Degrees of Separation. *In this drama, Smith plays a gay con artist who insinuates himself into the houses and lives of Park Avenue's most prominent people.*

one a degree of separation. Then he used the character of Paul, a gay con artist, to make audiences think about what actually separates people—race, age, class, education, sexual orientation—and about how easily those separations can be broken down by a skillful imposter.

The real culprit's motive was bilking his hosts of money, but in Guare's work money isn't really the point. Guare's main character is more interested in proving to wealthy individuals like New York City art dealers Ouisa and Flan Kittredge that, with the right clothes and manners, he is just as good as they are. In both the play and the movie, Paul first succeeds in getting the Kittredges' sympathy by pretending to be a college friend of their children's who has been mugged. He wins their trust with a display of intelligence, sophistication, and even gourmet cooking skills, revealing that he is Poitier's son.

The Kittredges are so impressed that they give Paul shelter and money, but then are horrified to find Paul in bed with another man and throw both men out of their home. Paul moves on to con other New Yorkers, eventually causing one victim to commit suicide and another to call the police. Ouisa, who has taken a motherly interest in Paul, tries to help him, but Paul is arrested and disappears into the justice system.

The movie *Six Degrees of Separation* would have moments of humor, but the overall message would be serious. The role of Paul called for a versatile actor who could be convincing as the imposter and as the "real" Paul, in the movie's final scene a poor, frightened street kid. Smith's challenge as Paul would be to make the audience sympathize with the con man while being appalled by him at the same time.

Enormous Challenges

Smith had played a homeless teen before so that didn't worry him. He also believed he could master polished, Harvard-educated speech because he had grown up practicing good grammar and diction. But Smith was intimated by a long, five-minute-plus monologue Guare had written for Paul. He wasn't confident that he could recite all those words and still stay convincingly in character.

And Smith was extremely uncomfortable with another aspect of the role: In one scene Paul appears in the nude and kisses another man. Smith's outspoken comments about his distaste for this scene caused homosexuals to label him homophobic. In an interview with *Cosmopolitan* magazine, Smith said, "Just the concept of looking at a man the way you'd look at a woman and saying to a man what you'd say to a woman was really hard. I don't have anything against homosexuals—I'm just not one."[46] He could draw on nothing from his own life to understand that part of Paul's personality, and he lacked the acting background to create such a character.

Worried, too, that his image as a cool rapper and ladies' man would suffer, Smith weighed the pros and cons of going after the role. In the end, he reasoned that playing someone so totally different from his public image was the best way to keep from being typecast.

Landing the Part

Smith told his agent to get him an audition, and then he began telling magazine and newspaper reporters that he wanted the

John Guare (pictured), author of the play Six Degrees of Separation, *initially refused to consider Smith for the role of Paul in the film version of the drama.*

part in *Six Degrees of Separation*. He hoped public buzz over his participation would boost his chances with the studio, and he campaigned just as hard to convince playwright Guare that he was the right man for the role. He knew that, even though Guare did not have absolute control in the movie's casting, his opinions would carry a great deal of weight.

At first Guare refused to even consider Smith. He scoffed at the idea that some silly kid on a comedy TV show could be Paul in his movie. Guare reports he kept saying, "I don't want to meet him [Will]. I don't need to. I have my cast."[47] In fact, Guare liked the actors who had done *Six Degrees* on Broadway so much that he had refused to sign a contract with MGM until they agreed that actress Stockard Channing would repeat her role as Ouisa Kittredge. He also wanted Courtney Vance to return as Paul, but he had to admit Vance was getting too old to play a college student.

Guare finally allowed himself to be talked into meeting with Smith on the set of *The Fresh Prince*. Smith worked hard to prepare

for this interview. He studied the movie script carefully and prepared a list of reasons why he should play Paul. But as it turned
out, the list wasn't necessary. Guare was immediately impressed
with Smith's wide range of interests and ready to sign him up.
Smith said, "He [Guare] walked into my dressing room, saw I
had a picture of Run DMC [a rap artist] next to one of Mao [for-
mer Chinese dictator], and he said, 'Oh my God, you're him,
you're Paul. You get it.'"[48]

With Guare on his side, Smith's next hurdle was convincing
director Fred Schepisi to give him a chance. Schepisi had interviewed dozens of candidates before he got to Smith, and he was
not enthusiastic about their meeting. Again Smith prepared to
sell himself as Paul. He wore a three-piece Brooks Brothers–type
suit to the interview and turned on the charm. When Schepisi
saw what a smooth salesman Smith could be, he quickly became
a believer. Stockard Channing said later that if Smith had shown
any doubt in his ability to portray Paul during that meeting, he
would not have gotten the part.

Becoming Paul

Smith spent the next three months preparing for the role. He
went to performances of the play in Los Angeles, New York, and
London to see how other actors portrayed Paul. He took acting
lessons and hired a speech coach. He started memorizing the
long monologue and working out so that he would look good in
the nude scene.

But in spite of all the preparations, Smith still had a few
doubts that he would really be able to pull off this role. Later he
told *Ebony,* "That was the first time I ever had to be someone
else. All of your instincts and all of the things that you've worked
on, all the faces you learn to make and all of your go-to tools
are stripped. And you're fighting a battle, but you can't use any
of the weapons that you've used your whole life."[49]

Smith was seriously fazed by the bedroom scene and asked
several friends for advice about it. Actor Denzel Washington
said he thought the part of Paul was a wonderful opportunity,
but he had mixed feelings about the kiss. Schepisi promised they
would postpone that scene until the final day of shooting, which

left Smith free to worry about forgetting lines during the long monologue. Stockard Channing told him to concentrate on being Paul and on the essence of what his character was saying rather than trying to get every single word right. That helped, but sometimes Smith got so into being Paul that this, too, became a problem. He said of that time, "Your lines of reality begin to blur. I'd speak like Paul and not realize it, and people would say, 'Why are you talking that way?'"[50]

In the end, Smith refused to shoot the kiss scene, which was instead simulated. Later Smith was ashamed of having been so unprofessional. He told *Ebony,* "You do the audience a disservice if you don't completely commit to the character. If you are not going to commit, don't take [the part]."[51]

Triumph

Even though Smith had a few reservations about his performance, when the movie came out in December 1993, it was soon obvious this role had been a wise choice. Instead of ridiculing him for playing a homosexual, his fellow rappers were impressed that he had gone after the part. The general public and the critics, although a little put off by the "talkiness" of the movie, still praised Smith's performance. Reviewer Michael J. Legeros said, "Then there's Smith. The young actor/rapper continues his upward spiral as a rising talent. He shows a nice range of emotions in the film's most dimensional role."[52]

A Favorite Board Game

When Smith was seven years old, his father taught him how to play chess. Being a competitive kid, Will worked at the game until he could beat his father. During the filming of *Six Degrees of Separation,* Smith found that his director, Fred Schepisi, also loved the game. They played match after match with the two being almost equally matched.

In a December 2001 interview with *Playboy,* Smith bragged that he rarely meets anyone who can beat him on a regular basis, but admitted that when he was making *Enemy of the State* one of the guys in the crew had beaten him badly. The next day Smith found a chess master and worked with this expert for the next three months until he could beat the crew member.

Smith assumed the role of Paul so completely that he had trouble keeping the impostor's character distinct from his own.

Critic James Berardinelli first acknowledged Stockard Channing's excellent work as Ouisa, then added, "The only other player of note is Will Smith, who shows that he can do more than the silly comedy of a weekly television program. Smith's Paul doesn't have the impact or strength of personality of Channing's Ouisa, but he never gets lost in the background."[53]

According to *Newsweek*, "Smith, the rapper and star of TV's *Fresh Prince of Bel-Air,* is an eyeopener in a complex, tricky part. That simple two syllable name is going to be very big."[54] They were right: *Six Degrees* completely changed the way directors and producers viewed Smith's potential as an actor. This movie opened the doors for the blockbuster roles that soon followed.

Chapter 5

Action Movie Hero

Once *Six Degrees of Separation* had convinced Hollywood that Smith could act, he was offered other interesting movie roles. He was eager to take on new challenges and to improve his acting skills, but he also had three more years on his *Fresh Prince* contract to fulfill.

And fulfilling that contract was beginning to feel like a chore. Not only was Smith anxious to get on with his plan to become a movie actor but, by the fourth season, he was having trouble identifying with his silly college-age TV character. As a husband and father, Smith now found his television counterpart's little scrapes terribly childish compared with his real-life concerns.

Smith's biggest concern was that his marriage was falling apart. Although he loved Sheree and their infant son, Trey, deeply, months went by when he hardly saw them. *Six Degrees of Separation* had kept him out of town for many weeks, and much of his free time in Los Angeles was spent with Townes recording the final album in their contract with Jive Records.

That album, called *Code Red,* was released in September 1993, but it failed to sell as well as Smith's other records. This perceived failure made him even more motivated to start focusing on things that really mattered. He couldn't keep juggling a family, a TV show, movie roles, and a music career with any success, so he decided that his music would have to go.

TV Show Problems

With the album out of the way, Smith turned his attention to his television show. He decided that if *The Fresh Prince* had better scripts, he would be more satisfied spending time on the set.

Bill Cosby (pictured) encouraged Smith to try his hand at scriptwriting after the young actor complained that The Fresh Prince *scripts were devoid of substance.*

He urged the show's writers to tackle more real-life issues instead of going for cheap laughs, but there was no dramatic change and Smith became more critical.

One night, when he was complaining to his friend Bill Cosby about the writing on *The Fresh Prince,* Cosby challenged Smith to see whether he could do any better. According to Smith, "Cosby suggested that I write a script." Cosby said, "Just write one and don't go to sleep until it's finished." Smith accepted the challenge and learned that writing was harder than he thought. He said, "When I met the writers the next day, I had a lot less anger and a lot more understanding of the process."[55]

But the lightweight scripts continued to bother Smith. He finally complained to Benny Medina, who promised Smith more input on what topics *The Fresh Prince* would address. That made Smith feel better, but it also made his writers angry enough to quit. Considering the turmoil behind the scenes, plus having a new actress on the set to play Aunt Viv, it looked as if the show was in trouble. However, new writers were hired, and Daphne

Maxwell Reid, the new Aunt Viv, fit right in with the rest of the cast. The show's ratings remained high.

Playing Against Type

When taping of the fourth season of *The Fresh Prince* ended, Smith was again free to take on a new movie role. This time he was chosen to costar in a buddy movie called *Bad Boys*. The original script had been written with *Saturday Night Live* stars Dana Carvey and Jon Lovitz in mind, but salary disputes and personality problems had stalled the project. At last coproducers Don Simpson and Jerry Bruckheimer gave up on their original idea and decided to use two black actors.

Luckily Mark Canton, head of Columbia Pictures, had seen *Six Degrees of Separation* and been sufficiently impressed with Smith's performance to want him for a movie. Canton was also interested in using black comic Martin Lawrence, and he figured that pairing these two television comedians instead of hiring more established movie stars would help to keep costs down. To him, this idea seemed like a gamble worth taking.

Simpson and Bruckheimer liked to gamble, too, so they cast Smith and Lawrence against image. Smith, who had always played the clean-cut, one-woman man on television and in real life, was assigned the part of Mike Lowery, the rich playboy cop. Lawrence's character would be the devoted family man, Marcus Burnett, not at all in line with the comedian's real-life reputation.

Smith leaped at the chance to be in this cops-and-robbers romp, and he said he saw the movie as a step forward for African Americans. He pointed out that, in *Bad Boys:* "Two black actors were in a film that was treated like a big-time film. Outside of Eddie Murphy and Whoopi Goldberg, you don't see this level of attention given to many films with black stars."[56]

Bad Boys, Bad Script

But even though this film was supposedly big-time, the plot of *Bad Boys* was thin. It concerned two loose cannon police officers who make a big drug bust, only to have the drugs stolen right out of the police lockup. Then, through a series of silly misunderstandings, the cops end up switching identities while baby-sitting a beautiful material witness to a murder.

Actually the plot was worse than weak; it was unfinished. There was no complete script when Smith and Lawrence arrived on the set, and no one seemed to know when they might expect to get one. Director Michael Bay was frantic, certain that his career was going to be ruined by such sloppy preparation.

But Bay soon realized that his two stars were quite capable of writing their own script as they went along. Their bonding was instantaneous, and they worked together beautifully. Smith said, "It never felt like we were strangers. The chemistry was really great. We basically ad-libbed every scene. It was two and a half months of two of the silliest guys in comedy doing exactly what they wanted to."[57]

Bad Boys was produced for a relatively cheap $20 million, partly because Smith and Lawrence did many of their own stunts. That was fine with Smith, but he brought along a large

Martin Lawrence (left) and Will Smith in a still from Bad Boys. *The script for the movie was unfinished when filming began, but the two actors were more than willing to ad-lib.*

friend of his from Philly and told Bay, "That's fine. I'll do all of the stunts, but the moment when my buddy here realizes I've been injured, he's been instructed to knock you out."[58]

Fresh Sex Symbol

From its opening weekend *Bad Boys* was a hit. It quickly brought in $15.5 million and continued to draw crowds. Besides proving Smith had box-office appeal, this movie also marked the first time he was described as sexy. *Entertainment Weekly* said of the picture, "Smith especially holds the camera with his matinee idol sexiness and his quicksilver delivery of lines."[59] Smith had long been known as a funny, charming, and thoroughly nice guy, but when this reporter said he was "sexy," women across the country agreed.

Sex appeal helped to boost his popularity with Hollywood casting directors, but the label had a downside for Smith personally. The more his fans wanted to throw themselves at him, the more unhappy Sheree was. Will was shocked and deeply hurt when she said she wanted a divorce. The couple discussed staying together, at least until Trey was older, but Sheree would not, and they divorced in December 1995.

Smith went through a low period, devastated by the failure of his marriage. He turned to friends for comfort, and one of those friends was a beautiful young actress named Jada Pinkett. With Pinkett, Will gradually saw better days ahead.

Saving the World

The first sign of those better days was when Smith's sexy new image got him a part in the science-fiction/action movie *Independence Day*. Smith had long wanted to try science fiction, observing years earlier that science-fiction films seemed especially profitable. He said, "I looked at the Top Ten movies of all time, seven of them had creatures in them: *E.T., Jurassic Park, Close Encounters of the Third Kind, Jaws*. It was like, Okay, let's make movies that have creatures in them."[60]

The creatures in *Independence Day* (often referred to as *ID4*) were aliens from outer space, the brainchildren of Roland Emmerich and Dean Devlin. Emmerich and Devlin had asked themselves what would happen if unfriendly alien spacecraft suddenly appeared over the world's major cities and started destroying civilization. To keep the audience guessing who would live and who would die in the movie, the cast of characters included several main heroes.

The first hero was the president of the United States, played by Bill Pullman. Another, played by Jeff Goldblum, was a computer genius with a plan to stop the aliens. Smith was hired to play the third hero, Air Force Captain Steven Hiller, who implements the plan. Emmerich and Devlin knew Smith could be brash and funny from his TV show. *Six Degrees of Separation* had convinced them he could also be serious, and *Bad Boys* had proved he had box-office appeal. They figured they could get 20th Century Fox to hire him for the part, and they were right.

Smith as a fighter pilot prepares to battle the alien force in Independence Day. *Aware of the blockbuster potential of science-fiction movies, Smith was eager to star in the film.*

So in the summer of 1995, Smith headed off to Utah "to save the world." He found this amusing and quipped, "Black people have been saving the world for years, and nobody knew it."[61] But he soon found that saving the world was hard work, especially in the Bonneville Salt Flats where temperatures reached 126 degrees Fahrenheit. Dragging a fake alien across the hot, shimmering sand for dozens of takes was downright exhausting.

And then there were the epic battles between Smith and figments of Emmerich's and Devlin's imaginations. Smith told *People* magazine, "In a scene with an alien, you're talking to air, or a sign that says 'ALIEN.'" For scenes inside the cockpit of the airplane, "the director stands off camera saying things like: 'There's an explosion on your left! Now the plane dips to your right!'" Smith says he thought, "Wait I never knew this is what Han Solo had to go through."[62]

But making *Independence Day* was not all hard work. In fact, the cast had so much fun with each other that Emmerich sometimes had trouble getting his stars to stop goofing off and get back to work. He said of Bill Pullman, Jeff Goldblum, Margaret Colin, Judd Hirsch, Randy Quaid, and Smith, "[they] liked each other so well that instead of going off to their trailers [during breaks], they would all stay around the set. . . . Everybody would start gossiping, and you'd have to say, 'Guys?' It was this ongoing party, and that was a problem during the whole movie."[63] For his part Smith was constantly staging mock ninja fights and having a great time.

Blockbuster

The film was barely finished before Emmerich was bragging about how smart he had been to give Smith top billing. He said of the test screenings, "Audiences identify with him—I'd see it in their eyes. . . . He's going to be huge."[64]

Shortly after Smith put the finishing touches on the final episode of the sixth season of *The Fresh Prince,* the buzz started to build that *ID4* was going to be a blockbuster. Twentieth Century Fox put on an impressive media blitz. Then on Fourth of July weekend in 1996, *ID4* opened its run by grossing over $92 million, making it the most successful film debut in history. For several years, *ID4* even held a place as the third-highest money maker of all time, trailing only *Titanic* and *Jurassic Park*. Suddenly Smith was a box-office star.

Spielberg Calling

All this hoopla meant that Smith was deluged by movie offers. He tried to be cool and noncommittal while considering his options until famed director Stephen Spielberg called to tap Smith for a hip sci-fi spoof called *Men in Black (MIB)*. At first Smith thought someone was playing a practical joke on him, and Spielberg had a hard time convincing him that the call was for real. According to Smith, Spielberg said, "You have to do this movie. We don't even want to talk about it." As Smith put it, "You just can't tell Steven Spielberg no."[65] So he signed on to the project for $5 million and an undisclosed amount for writing the movie's rap theme song.

With Tommy Lee Jones playing the special agent who recruits Smith to save the world from dazzlingly designed space aliens, Smith donned a dark suit and tie, white shirt, Ray-Ban sunglasses, and a deadpan expression. Then Jones and Smith and their heavy-duty, three-barrel alien-blasting guns went to work to keep those aliens at bay, innocent bystanders in the dark, and the audience in stitches.

Smith and Jones worked well together, even though Jones had a prickly reputation. At times, it appeared they belonged to a mutual admiration society. Smith said of Jones:

> We had a ball on the set of this movie. I know it might be hard to believe, but Tommy Lee Jones is actually a comedic genius. He really understands comedy to a technical level that very few people understand. Deadpan delivery is the most difficult, but he can do it because he does nothing; he just says the words. For me that's perfect. And with that dead-straight delivery [of his], he would toss me soft pitches that I could smack out of the ballpark.[66]

In response, Jones said he'd figured out the way to be funny was to just stand as close to Will Smith as possible.

Tommy Lee Jones (left) and Smith in a scene from Men in Black. *The two actors worked very well together during filming of the sci-fi spoof.*

Of course not every day on the set was fun, and the worst was the day they shot a scene in which a giant bug explodes after it is shot. Smith and Jones were drenched with a lumpy glycerine slime that got in their noses and mouths. It was truly disgusting, but a movie star does what he has to do.

A Second Blockbuster

Possibly an actor's tensest moments are spent waiting for a new movie to open. But in 1997, one year after *Independence Day* opened on Fourth of July weekend to huge box-office sales, *Men in Black* was declared a blockbuster as well. Over its first six days, *MIB* earned $84.1 million, and it ranked for several years as the ninth-highest grossing movie in history. Even the critics generally liked this one. *USA Today* gave it four stars, the highest possible rating, and said, "*MIB* is kind of *Independence Day* for smart people. Smith is so appealingly cool it should be illegal."[67]

Men in Black cemented Smith's reputation as an actor who could bring in moviegoers by the hundreds of thousands, and it even reignited his music career. The movie's soundtrack featuring his rap theme song topped the *Billboard* Hot 100 Singles list for four weeks straight. Columbia Records was so impressed that they quickly signed him to a recording contract.

Smith's contract for his TV show had run out in the spring of 1996, which left him enough free time to record again. His new album *Big Willie Style* was released in November 1996. It was his first album under his own name rather than as Fresh Prince, and it produced two huge hits. "Just the Two of Us" is a sweet and clever rap about fatherhood and "Gettin' Jiggy Wit It" is a return to the fun dance music he and Townes started with. Television sitcom star Jerry Seinfeld picked up on the phrase "getting jiggy" and used it on his top-rated show, which helped to boost album sales. *Big Willie Style* went platinum only a month after its release.

Smith had charted a course to become a big star and followed it. Now he redefined his goal. From this point on he told everyone he wanted to be the most versatile entertainer in Hollywood.

Chapter 6

Becoming More Versatile

After three consecutive hit movies, Smith had a solid reputation as an actor and plenty of money in the bank. He could now afford to take some risks in his quest to become a truly versatile actor.

At first glance his next movie, *Enemy of the State,* was a variation of the two blockbusters Smith had just finished. Although all three previous movies feature lots of shoot-outs and special effects, *Enemy* offered him new challenges. In the latter movie, he plays a much more serious character who is on his own against the crooks.

Smith plays a good-citizen Manhattan lawyer named Robert Dean who gets caught up in a government conspiracy. When a hot-potato videotape showing the murder of a congressman by a National Security Agency (NSA) operative is planted on him, his life suddenly starts falling apart. At first he is unaware he even has the tape, but NSA will stop at nothing to retrieve the evidence and make sure Dean doesn't talk.

The lawyer tries to run, but an endless array of NSA surveillance gadgets keep finding him. Dean loses his wife's trust, his bank account, and most of his clothing trying to shed bugs. About halfway through the movie Dean finally gets some help from a quirky character called Brill, and the hero sets out to turn the tables. *Enemy of the State* called for big name talent to carry the film.

Indeed, it was rumored that one of the biggest names in Hollywood, Tom Cruise, was offered the role of Robert Dean before Smith. Director Tony Scott, however, insists that he had

Smith in mind from the beginning. Scott said, "I had looked at Will Smith in *Six Degrees of Separation*. . . . I also looked at bits of *Bad Boys, Independence Day* and *Men in Black* when he had a few serious moments, and he handled them so well and his choices during those moments were so good, I knew he could handle something more serious."[68] The show's producer, Jerry Bruckheimer, agreed.

Bruckheimer and Scott also agreed they wanted Gene Hackman to play Brill, a jaded operative with dubious ethics who deals in underground information and high-tech surveillance. Their logic was obvious. Hackman had played similar characters in *The Conversation* and *The French Connection,* for which he won an Oscar.

Smith was delighted to hear that he'd be working with the highly respected Hackman, whose stature he aspired to: "The way to be great is to associate with greatness. You hang out with Oscar winners, and people start to think you belong there."[69]

But when it was time to start shooting, Smith got a little nervous knowing he would be largely responsible for the success or failure of the $90 million movie. He told *Jet Magazine*, "It's the first time that I've been completely out front, where the show is about my character. It's not just physically exhausting, the emotional aspect can be equally daunting."[70]

Smith in a dramatic scene from Enemy of the State. *Smith plays a lawyer caught in the middle of a government cover-up of a congressman's murder.*

Gene Hackman (right) stars with Smith in Enemy of the State. *Smith considered it a high honor to work with the acclaimed veteran actor.*

Smith wanted to do his best work, so he asked several people for advice on how to play Robert Dean. One was his girlfriend Jada, who introduced Smith to her uncle, a real-life Baltimore lawyer. Smith saw that Jada's uncle could be dead serious about business one minute and cracking jokes with his family the next. Jada's uncle became the role model for Robert Dean.

Touring the CIA

Filming of *Enemy of the State* began in Baltimore, Maryland, in the fall of 1997. Since the fictitious National Security Agency is patterned after the CIA, the movie's producers arranged for Smith to take a four-hour tour of CIA headquarters in Virginia. He probably expected the people who worked in this spy headquarters to be close mouthed and standoffish, but such was not the case. During Smith's entire visit he was busy signing autographs. He took such requests in stride, but he was appalled to learn that the real CIA had surveillance capabilities far beyond the scary devices in his movie.

The thought of someone actually watching his every move and conspiring against him gave Smith the creeps. He told *Rolling Stone,* "I'm definitely a conspiracy theorist, and *Enemy of the State* only confirmed my beliefs."[71] When the movie was completed it would give its viewers the same eerie feeling.

Everyman

Throughout the high-tech plot twists, car chases, and explosions, Smith managed to portray the image of a normal, everyday guy caught up in events beyond his control. He played this everyman character with such skill that critics began to compare him to some of Hollywood's greatest actors.

For example, when the movie came out in 1998, Steve Murray of the *Atlanta Journal* called Smith a "street-smart Cary Grant."[72] Peter Travers of *Rolling Stone* said that in casting Smith as the besieged young lawyer,

> [Bruckheimer] borrows a trick from the master, Alfred Hitchcock, who knew you had to cast a star—say, Jimmy Stewart [in] *The Man Who Knew Too Much* or Cary Grant [in] *North By Northwest*—whom the audience would follow anywhere. Bruckheimer and director Tony Scott have wisely set their course by Will Smith, who is sensational in a dramatic role that leans on him to carry a movie without the help of aliens or Big Willie–style jokes for every occasion.[73]

Smith had proved once more that he could handle a serious role as well as comedy.

Jada

Smith took on a serious commitment in his personal life about that time, too. On New Year's Eve of 1997, he married Jada Pinkett in a wedding extravaganza rumored to have cost over $3 million. A few days later they were delighted to learn that Jada was pregnant. The expectant couple set up housekeeping in Smith's Spanish-style hacienda set on four acres of oasis in Thousand Oaks, California. The home featured a pool, a recording studio, a par-three golf course, and three Rottweilers. (Two of these dogs had been gifts from his pal Jay Leno.)

The new couple's most frequent houseguests were Trey and his mother, Sheree. Smith says that this closeness with his for-

Jada

Will first met Jada in 1990 when she auditioned to play his girlfriend on *The Fresh Prince*. She didn't get the part because at five feet tall, the show's producers felt she was too short for Will, who stands six feet two inches.

But in those days Jada's acting was much better than Will's, because she had studied her craft at the Baltimore School for the Arts. Shortly after she failed to get on *The Fresh Prince*, she was hired to play Lena James on *A Different World*. Roles in movies such as *Menace II Society*, *Scream 2*, and *The Nutty Professor* soon followed.

When Will first saw Jada, he thought that she was very attractive, but she thought he was just goofy. In the following years, Will and Jada rubbed elbows at various social events, but they never really talked until after Will's 1995 divorce. Then one night in 1996, they found themselves at a dinner party for eight, and the only unmarried guests. Paired at the dinner, they talked; Will opened up about his pain in having failed at marriage and Jada told Will about her failed relationship with basketball star Grant Hill. From that night on they began to see each other in a different light and spent time together trying to sort out their lives. Soon they had fallen deeply in love.

mer wife and his son was all Jada's doing. "She worked it out with Sheree," he reports, "which helped me be the best father I could be for Trey."[74]

Smith became a father for the second time in July 1998. He and Jada called their new son Jaden Christopher Syre Smith, and again Will felt the weight of fatherhood. At the time Smith said, "Having two kids, it's like I'm a real dad now. I took it seriously before, but now there's a whole other dynamic that kicks in. Now, I gotta really go to work."[75]

Fun on the Set

But he had so much fun making his next movie, *Wild Wild West*, that it barely qualified as work. His old pal Barry Sonnenfeld, who had directed *Men in Black*, was again in charge and Smith's character was something like James Bond in a cowboy hat. Agent James West had all the answers, and he always got the girl.

The movie was based on the popular 1960s television series starring Robert Conrad. George Clooney was at first slated to play Agent West with Smith as his sidekick, Artemus Gordon.

However, Smith was given the lead when Clooney backed out, and the new sidekick was Kevin Kline.

The story is set in the years just after the Civil War with the Secret Service agent heroes working directly for President Ulysses S. Grant. Their goal is to stop the evil Dr. Arliss Loveless from assassinating the president and taking over the country. Loveless uses a batch of incredible science-fiction–type inventions to help him in his evil plots, and West and Gordon counter with crazy contraptions of their own.

The story line of the movie was nutty enough, but sometimes the off-camera action was just as crazy. One day director Sonnenfeld was fooling around with Smith, and the director got hurt. The studio claimed it happened when a stage door flew open unexpectedly, but others said Sonnenfeld and Smith had been staging a fake boxing match. When Sonnenfeld's punch missed, he hit Smith's shoulder bone and broke his wrist. In spite of this mishap and a fire that broke out on one of the sets, the movie got finished and everyone expected *Wild Wild West* to be a big hit.

Blockbuster Expected

Believing it had a blockbuster on its hands, Warner Brothers studio gave it even more advance publicity than usual. It made deals with food manufacturers to capitalize on the film's expected success. Burger King prepared millions of plastic figures and kiddie sunglasses to tie in with the movie's release. Dreyer's Ice Cream came up with a special flavor of its product with things that looked like Dr. Loveless's giant spider imbedded in it. Everyone connected with the movie eagerly awaited the Fourth of July holiday weekend and certain success.

Hype plays a big role in selling a movie to the public, but if the movie is bad enough, nothing can save it. Unfortunately *Wild Wild West* was called that bad. Many critics said they wanted to like the movie because Will Smith was in it, but that the film's story line was just too silly. People also found it hard to believe that a black man had recently survived the Civil War and was already an experienced government employee. Others were less interested in watching Smith play a man with all the answers than when he portrayed someone more vulnerable.

Whatever the reasons, the negative feedback on *Wild Wild West* started before it ever hit the theaters. It began when test audiences gave the film a surprisingly poor rating. Director Barry Sonnenfeld angrily defended his movie by blaming Warner Brothers for bungling things. He said the test audiences had been told they were going to see *The Matrix,* and when *Wild Wild West*'s title frame came on the screen, some of them actually booed. After such a deception, they weren't likely to give the movie a fair chance.

Hammered by the Critics

But the critics were just as negative about *Wild Wild West* at their preview events. Having been asked when he first knew the movie was in trouble, Smith said, "Probably at the press junket, after the reporters had seen the film. I have a fairly good relationship with the media, so a lot of guys who rip other people kind of take it easy on me. On *Wild Wild West* the first question [after the viewing was, 'So, when are you working on *Men in Black 2*?]"[76]

Other critics were less polite. The *Washington Post* summed it up when they said, "Waste of time. Waste of money, and a colossal waste of talent."[77]

Kevin Kline (left) and Smith in a scene from Wild Wild West. *The action comedy was not a critical success.*

Smith and his family at the premiere of Wild Wild West. *Despite negative press, the film did well at the box office and pleased Smith's loyal fans.*

In spite of the bad press, Smith's fans made *Wild Wild West* one of the top-grossing films for its opening weekend. Their loyalty actually made him feel worse. He said, "My fans and I have an unspoken understanding that I don't put out no dookie. . . . People come out in droves the first weekend and make me look like a big star. *Wild Wild West* had a $52 million opening weekend, number one movie, and it killed me because I knew it was wack. I felt like I had cheated my fans."[78]

Not everyone hated the movie, but the committee that gives out the so-called Razzies certainly did. Those are the dubious awards for the worst of everything in a given year. In 1999, *Wild Wild West* won for the worst picture, worst director, worst screenplay, worst song, and worst screen couple (Smith and Kline).

A More Subdued Role

But Smith didn't let bad reviews stop him from taking on an even more unusual part. In *The Legend of Bagger Vance* he would not be funny, heroic, or even sexy. Instead, he would be sub-

dued and respectful as the mystical servant of the main character in a movie about golf. The director would be Robert Redford, and his costar teen idol Matt Damon.

According to the movie's story line, Matt Damon's character, Rannulph Junuh, once had the potential to be the greatest
golfer in history. But after serving in World War I, Junuh has returned to Georgia a ruined man. He has lost his wife, his will to
live, and obviously the will to play golf.

His wife, played by Charlize Theron, is a feisty woman who
still loves Junuh, and she has a plan to get him back. She orga-
nizes a golf match between the most famous men of the day and
challenges Junuh to play as the local favorite. He resists her efforts to pull him out of his despair until a mysterious, near-
divine character named Bagger Vance wanders into town and
gives Junuh a new lease on life.

Smith joked that one of the reasons he wanted to do this
movie was that he "dug the idea of being in a movie full of white
people where the only black man turns out to be God."[79]

The screenplay was based on a novel by Steven Pressfield,
and the novel was based on a Hindu story about a wise prophet.
Director Redford decided to make Bagger Vance less of a prophet
and more of a trickster who inspires people to help themselves.
Smith liked this change because it allowed him to add a little
humor to the part. He said, "I'm still funny but in a more subtle,
less direct kind of way. That way I could maintain that relationship I've had with my fans since *Fresh Prince of Bel-Air*."[80]

But playing the part of Bagger Vance soon caused him to realize that life as a black man in the South in the 1930s was anything but funny. He began to realize a little about what
segregation and racial prejudice must have been like before the
civil rights battles. He told Terry Lawson of the *Detroit Free Press,*
"You step into those shoes for a while, even in a movie, and you
realize how heroic it was for a man to maintain his dignity and
sense of self under those circumstances."[81]

It was hard for Smith to subdue his buoyant personality. He
told CNN that he had to keep restraining his natural instincts to
go for the humor or steal the scene. He had to keep reminding
himself that *Bagger Vance* was not that kind of movie. On the

Matt Damon (right) and Smith in a still from The Legend of Bagger Vance. *Playing the role of Bagger Vance gave Smith an appreciation for the plight of the southern black man in the 1930s.*

other hand, for Smith the golf nut, being on a golf course every day was the next best thing to heaven. He said that he had never had so much fun making a movie.

More Criticism

Smith could be thankful that *Bagger Vance* had been fun to make, because as it turned out, reviewers found little to praise. Critics laid most of the blame on the story line. Peter Travers of *Rolling Stone* said, "Personally, I'd rather slice into the deep rough than have some mystical caddie blowing hot air in my ear about the symbolic meaning of my golf swing."[82] Richard von Busack was equally disgusted with the point of the movie. He said, "It's as if Smith's trying to hypnotize the audience into a state where it'll believe this New Age gunk unquestioningly."[83]

Director Spike Lee, however, attacked Smith personally for taking this role: "In real life, black men were being castrated and lynched left and right. With all that going on, why are you [expletive deleted] trying to teach Matt Damon a golf swing?"[84] Smith had been criticized before for not speaking out on racial issues. Perhaps his next movie about the life of a truly heroic black man would silence those critics.

Chapter 7

Ali and Beyond

Smith had long admired former heavyweight boxing champion Muhammad Ali, and he knew that portraying Ali on the screen could be the role of a lifetime. But back in the early 1990s, when he was first asked to play this international icon and African-American hero, Smith had to say no. He doubted that his acting skills were up to the job, and he had no idea how to prepare for such a role. Neither was he ready to make such a huge commitment of his time and energy at that point in his life.

Columbia/Sony Pictures, however, kept asking. They felt that Smith's box-office appeal, physical size, and good looks, which rivaled the retired boxer's, made him the logical choice. They had seen that Smith could be serious and heroic as well as funny. Even his playful rap lyrics were similar to the rhymes Ali once used to taunt his opponents.

Smith understood the similarities, and as his acting improved, the role might have seemed more possible to him. However, in the mid 1990s, his divorce from Sheree Zampino had left him too emotionally bruised to seek new challenges. He worried that preparing himself to portray Ali would be even more difficult than his work for *Six Degrees of Separation* and he blamed all those months away from Sheree for the failure of his marriage. He would not risk losing Jada Pinkett, too.

Being a Father

Neither did Smith want Trey to feel abandoned, because he felt an awesome responsibility to be a good father. When Trey was five years old, Will wrote a beautiful rap poem about fatherhood called "Just the Two of Us." To this day Smith feels it is the best thing he ever wrote, and many people agree. "Just the Two of Us" was part of the 1997 hit album *Big Willie Style* and his video of the single won numerous awards. In 2001, the poem was published as a children's book, and this, too, was a huge success. *Library Talk* said, "An incredible picture book. . . . He [Smith] tenderly touches on everything from car seats to manners. . . . This book is destined to be a classic tribute to fathers and sons."[85]

The Ideal Wife

If any woman was to have a future with Smith, she would have to love Trey, and Jada Pinkett was more than qualified. An experienced actor in her own right, she was also blessed with sensational good looks, common sense, warmth, and the ability to fit in with all kinds of people; but the thing Smith admired most was her incredible strength of character. He says, "There's a real ghetto edge to Jada. There's a strength that women of oppression possess that, once you remove the insecurities of that op-

Smith and his wife, Jada Pinkett Smith, pose with beaming smiles. Smith attributes his attraction to Jada to her strength and independence.

pression, there's an individual who can take you anywhere, support you in anything, carry you. . . . That strength is really sexy to me. It draws at the deepest pit of my being."[86]

Pinkett, a strong and independent woman, also learned to cherish her role as Will's helpmate. She added Smith to her stage name, and on November 2, 2000, she gave birth to their second child, a girl they named Willow Camille Reign Smith. With Jada at his side, Will felt like a winner in his personal life.

Returning to Music

In 1999, his music was also winning him new fans. *Big Willie Style* had eventually reached the 9X platinum designation, and *Willennium,* released in November, had already gone double platinum by December. Smith's last two movies, however, had been disappointments. It was time for him to get back on track as an actor.

About the same time the *Ali* project was at last nearing the filming stage, since copyright issues had been settled. The script had been cut to focus on only the most dramatic years of the boxer's life, from 1964 to 1974. A new director had been chosen, and then Muhammad Ali called and personally asked Smith to do this movie.

The Curriculum

What could Smith say? He agreed to talk to director Michael Mann, and Mann showed him a workable plan for getting the movie made. As Smith recalls it, Mann said,

> "I will prepare the the curriculum you need." It was the first time I actually saw the road. I had never seen the successful route to making *Ali.* And then Michael talked me through it—it was a long, raggedy, jagged, dangerous road up the side of a mountain. In the rain. I knew I had to be a superhero to actually walk that road, but at least I could see it.[87]

A few weeks later Smith started running up that road, through the mountains of Colorado in heavy combat boots to build up his strength. He lifted weights and spent time with a punching bag to gradually put on thirty pounds of hard muscle so that he could look and perform like a boxer. He also read volumes on the Muslim religion and Ali's life. He watched hours of videotapes of Ali in action. Dialect coaches drilled him on the unique rhythms and telltale pronunciations of Ali's speech.

But above all, Smith struggled to learn how to box. Since Mann refused to use doubles or trick photography for the fight scenes, Smith would have to defend himself. And merely learning how to box wasn't enough. He had to copy Ali's exact boxing style to please boxing fans who remembered the fights he

Getting the Ali Look

Ali director Michael Mann was determined to make Smith look as much like the young Muhammad Ali as possible. Besides having his star beef up with thirty extra pounds of muscle to match Ali's fighting weight, the director instructed Columbia Pictures' makeup department to work on Smith's face and hair.

The first goal was to change the way Smith's trademark ears stuck out from his head. The solution was a prosthetic mold, which took an hour and a half to put in place each day. Once his ears were pinned back, Smith no longer looked like himself.

The actor's forehead was higher than the champion's, so a partial hairpiece was used. Instead of his usual hairstyle, Smith let his hair grow out and curl. Smith's nose was also given heavy makeup to complete the transformation.

Muhammad Ali (center) with his gold medal at the 1960 Olympics.

Smith raises his arm in victory in a scene from Ali. *The young actor meticulously imitated Ali's boxing style to enhance his credibility in the role.*

would be reenacting. Smith says, "He [Mann] even had a neuro-biologist come on the set to explain the inner workings of the human brain and what I could do to create neuropathways that'd help me fight more like Ali."[88]

Then came the practice fights. Smith, the actor, will never forget the first day he slugged it out with a real heavyweight boxer. When he momentarily let down his guard a huge fist landed on the side of his head. He said of the experience, "Have you ever put your tongue on a 9-volt battery? That was the taste I had in my mouth. There was a bright blue flash that faded to black. I don't know how to describe it, but there was the sound—whooo-ohhh-whoo."[89]

That was a bad day, but there were fun days, too, especially when Muhammad Ali came to visit the mining camp. Smith and the former champ liked to tease each other about who was the prettiest. Actually, the makeup department had succeeded in making Smith look very much like Ali, but trying to keep every-thing in place while he boxed was difficult.

Another challenge awaited him, too. He had never before been asked to do a serious bedroom scene, and this movie called for one. Smith was relieved when Jada was hired to play Ali's first wife so he could do the love scene with her.

The Trip to Africa

After months of preparation, the cameras began rolling for *Ali*. Things went well until it was time to go to Africa to recreate "The Rumble in the Jungle," the last big fight of Ali's career. Sony Pictures, aware that the film was going over budget, refused to pay for the trip. Mann felt the movie needed this taste of Africa to give it authenticity, so he and his aides searched for more financing. They secured some money, but it was still not enough.

That is when Smith asked himself exactly how committed he was to making this movie the best it could be. He thought about what Ali's story could mean to people younger than himself, especially African Americans, who probably didn't know about the fighter's early years. Smith wanted them to be aware of the sacrifices Ali had made to stand up for his rights. Then he decided to put up his $20 million salary as guarantee against the possibility of Sony losing money on the picture. When Michael Mann followed suit, Smith and his crew were off to Africa.

Landing in Maputo, Mozambique, was an emotional experience for Smith, a reaction Smith's friend and costar Jamie Foxx maintains is not unusual among African Americans: "The thing with black people [is], we've always wanted to come back to Africa."[90] Smith said of the landing:

> I [had] a tornado of emotions. When we first got off the plane one of the baggage handlers said, "Welcome home, Brother," and I was done. I was like [covering his eyes as if crying] "All us American brothers ain't soft like this, Brother, just let me get this out and I'm gonna talk to you in a moment."[91]

Later Smith told interviewers that being in Africa had a profound effect on him. A *USA Today* article reported that he wanted to spend more time educating himself about Africa and that he even planned to buy a home on the continent "to enhance his understanding of his roots and to provide his sons with a sense of ancestry."[92]

Rap Music in Africa

While Smith was in Africa, he was amazed to learn that his rap music was popular there—even in villages with no electricity—and troubled at the realization that in many areas of the world, rap music might be the people's sole source of information about black Americans.

Smith said that one girl, in particular, was terribly afraid of him. She refused to come near him the entire time he was in her village because she expected him to have a gun and try to hurt her. This experience made him more determined than ever to work for more responsible rap lyrics among his peers.

Comments Smith made on the weekly newsmagazine *Prime Time* indicate some naiveté on Smith's part. His preconceived image of modern Africa did not include forty-story buildings and beautiful girls driving BMWs, and he was amazed to hear rap music.

The Africans knew more about Smith than he knew about them. He was hailed as a conquering hero, everywhere the center of much enthusiasm. Sometimes the people of Mozambique got carried away, however; the night the crew shot the final fight scene of the movie, sixty-five thousand people showed up to serve as extras. Many had seats inside the auditorium, but many more were kept outside where they drank lots of local beer. Visions of people getting trampled in mass hysteria haunted the moviemakers. Indeed, one of these rowdies threw a bottle that almost killed a twelve-year-old boy. Fortunately, the boy survived and this final scene did get filmed.

Smith enjoyed being in Africa so much that he hated to leave, but he had to get back to Hollywood to deal with all the publicity appearances for the movie. For the next few months he was kept busy promoting the film in print and broadcast interviews and public appearances.

The Response to *Ali*

Ali was released on December 25, 2001, grossing $10.2 million on Christmas Day, second only to *Lord of the Rings* in box-office sales. But when the holiday weekend was over, *Ali* was not deemed a Will Smith blockbuster. Critics and the general public alike said that although the fight scenes were well staged, the movie itself failed to reveal who Ali, the man, really was. Some blamed the script; others blamed director Michael Mann.

Todd McCarthy of *Variety* said, "The filmmaker's brooding personality and style have imposed themselves on Muhammad Ali more than Ali's zest and impudence have loosened up Mann, resulting in a picture that feels bottled up."[93]

On the other hand, there was high praise for Smith's acting. McCarthy concluded, "Smith carries the picture with consummate skill."[94] *People* magazine called Smith "impressive."[95] Peter Travers of *Rolling Stone* was even more enthusiastic. He said, "Smith gives a towering performance, defiantly funny and impassioned."[96] Travers went on to suggest that the performance was worthy of an Oscar.

Muhammad Ali (left) and Smith jab playfully at the Hollywood premiere of Ali, *as Smith's son Trey looks on.*

In fact, *Ali* earned Smith Academy Award and Golden Globe nominations for best actor, although he won neither. Keeping any disappointment private, Smith said the making of *Ali* had been about more important things: "I've been to my physical, mental, emotional, spiritual, and financial limits. I know who I am now. And this film made it more transparent to me who I want to be."[97]

Who Is That?

So who does Smith want to be? These days his dreams go far beyond being a Hollywood actor: He wants to be someone who has made the world a better place. In a *Prime Time* interview he said, "There's a really bittersweet emotion that I feel from playing this role that I'll never be that great. I want to be important. I want the world to be different because I was here, however lofty or crazy or delusional that may sound. I want some people's lives to be better because I was here."[98]

In part that means sharing his millions with the less fortunate. Even before coming to Hollywood, he was generous with his friends, and once he got past his troubles with the IRS, he again began to contribute money to causes he believed in. For example, he has financially helped the careers of several novice black athletes and entertainers. When he was on location for *The Legend of Bagger Vance,* Smith donated money to improve poor schools in Georgia. After he and Jada were married, they set up the Will and Jada Smith Family Foundation to help children in the ghettos of Philadelphia and Baltimore.

But Smith believes in doing more than donating money in his quest to improve the world. In the December 2001 issue of *InStyle* magazine, he said, "I think acting is just a pit stop on the road to my true calling."[99] Part of that calling has been to serve as a positive role model for young people and to portray African American youth in a favorable light. His rap music has served that purpose, and in 1996 he took part in the Million Man March while helping Spike Lee finance a movie about this meeting of responsible African American men. In 2001, Smith appeared at Russell Simmons's Hip-Hop Summit where Nation of Islam leader Louis Farrakhan told that gathering of rap artists,

"With leadership comes responsibility . . . if you can't inspire people to be positive and be leaders and dream, you're not utilizing the power that you have for the best."[100]

What lies ahead for Will Smith? His sequel to *Men in Black* hits theaters in the summer of 2002, and *Bad Boys 2* is scheduled for release in 2003. Among other projects rumored to be in his future are a movie with Jada called *Kind Hearts and Coronets;* a film version of John Grisham's best-selling novel *The Runaway Jury;* a remake of *A Star Is Born;* a screenplay Will and Jada wrote called *Love for Sale;* and a Ben Affleck story called *Affirmative Action.* Smith has been mentioned as the possible

Smith Is Sometimes Too Open with the Press

One of Will Smith's greatest assets is his approachability. He doesn't put on airs and he's never evasive when asked a question. This trait makes him immensely popular with talk-show hosts as well as with reporters and fans.

But this openness also gets him in trouble. For example, when making *Six Degrees of Separation* he confided to reporters that he found kissing another man in his role as a homosexual to be too awful to consider. Soon throngs of homosexuals were condemning him for being homophobic. Smith also quoted Denzel Washington as having told him the kiss was a bad idea, which forced Washington to defend his own statement to the press.

When Janet Hubert-Whitten was fired from *The Fresh Prince of Bel-Air,* she said nasty things about Smith and blamed him for her having lost her job. Smith angrily retorted that she just wanted to be the star of his show. Evidently that got Smith in hot water, too, because not long after that he was quoted as saying Ms. Hubert-Whitten was an incredible actress who brought great warmth to the set.

As recently as 2001, Smith put his foot in his mouth again. When a reporter asked him how he felt about his place in Hollywood today, Smith complained that he was getting only the scripts that Tom Hanks and Tom Cruise turned down and that he hoped someday the opposite would be true.

The media gleefully reported that Smith was taunting his competitors. So, in almost every interview he gave to promote his movie *Ali,* he also had to explain that this remark had been a joke and that actually he thought highly of Hanks and Cruise.

Smith looking dapper at the premiere of The Legend of Bagger Vance. *Smith is poised to extend the success he enjoyed in the twentieth century well into the twenty-first.*

lead in a planned film about the life of Nelson Mandela, but Smith says he is not interested because it would put too big a strain on his family.

In addition to acting, Smith owns several movie production companies, and he may try his hand at directing. His interest in rap music and rap videos remains strong.

And perhaps Smith will one day leave Hollywood in his quest to make people's lives better. Reflecting boundless enthusiasm for new challenges, he has said on many occasions that an eventual run for the presidency of the United States is not out of the question.

Many of Smith's friends believe he can do anything he sets his mind to. From their earliest days of working together, Jazzy Jeff saw that here was someone who could never be satisfied with the status quo. Jeff once remarked, "If Will came to me and said he wanted to be the first rapper/actor on the moon, I'd be the first one to go out and get me a spacesuit. Whatever Will says he's gonna do, he does."[101]

Notes

Chapter 1: A Solid Base to Jump From

1. Quoted in Lynn Norment, "Will Smith," *Ebony,* August 1996, p. 39.
2. Quoted in Nancy Collins, "Will Smith," *Rolling Stone,* December 1, 1998, p. 67.
3. Quoted in David Ritz, "Will Power," *Essence,* February 1993, p. 60.
4. Quoted in *Ebony Man,* "Will Smith," September 1996, p. 62.
5. Quoted in Mike Sager, "The Fresh King," *Vibe,* September 1998, p. 134.
6. Quoted in *Ebony Man,* "Will Smith," p. 62.
7. Quoted in Michael Fleming, "Will Smith," *Playboy,* December 2001, p. 171.
8. Quoted in Collins, "Will Smith," p. 66.
9. Quoted in Gregory Cerio, "Mister Smith Goes to Stardom," *People,* September 22, 1996, p. 69.
10. Quoted in Sager, "Fresh King," p. 133.
11. Quoted in Brian J. Robb, *King of Cool: Will Smith.* London: Plexus, 2000, p. 14.
12. Quoted in Norment, "Will Smith," p. 34.
13. Quoted in Fleming, "Will Smith," p. 72.
14. Quoted in Chris Nickson, *Will Smith.* New York: St. Martin's, 1999, p. 15.
15. Quoted in Francelia Sevin, "A Talk with Will Smith," *Scholastic Update,* September 1991, p. 24.
16. Quoted in Norment, "Will Smith," p. 38.

Chapter 2: The Fresh Prince of Philadelphia

17. Quoted in Quincy Jones, *Q.* New York: Doubleday, 2001, p. 279.
18. Interview with Terry Gross on *Fresh Air,* National Public Radio, November 27, 2001.

19. Quoted in Brian J. Robb, *King of Cool*, p. 17.
20. Quoted in Anne Janette Johnson, "Personal Information," June 1991. vol. 5. www.members.austarmetro.com.
21. Quoted in Collins, "Will Smith," p. 65.
22. Quoted in Collins, "Will Smith," p. 67.
23. Quoted in Brian J. Robb, *King of Cool*, p. 27.
24. Quoted in Jeffrey Ressner, "No Nightmares of D.J. Jazzy Jeff & the Fresh Prince," *Rolling Stone*, December 1, 1988, p. 19.
25. Quoted in K.S. Rodriguez, *Will Smith: From Fresh Prince to King of Cool*. New York: HarperCollins, 1998, p. 20.
26. Quoted in Rodriguez, *Will Smith*, p. 24.
27. Quoted in Collins, "Will Smith," p. 67.
28. Quoted in Nickson, *Will Smith*, p. 35.
29. Quoted in Collins, "Will Smith," p. 68.
30. Quoted in Nickson, *Will Smith*, p. 38.

Chapter 3: The Fresh Prince of Bel-Air

31. Quoted in Laura B. Randolph, "The Real-Life Fresh Prince of Bel-Air," *Ebony*, April 1991, p. 34.
32. Quoted in Randolph, "The Real-Life Fresh Prince of Bel-Air," p. 38.
33. Quoted in Nickson, *Will Smith*, p. 44.
34. Quoted in Gregory Cerio, "Mister Smith Goes to Stardom," *People*, September 22, 1996, p. 64.
35. Quoted in Fleming, "Will Smith," p. 62.
36. Quoted in Mary Murphy, "Rap 'n' Rhyme with the Prince of Prime Time," *TV Guide*, October 1990, p. 9.
37. Quoted in Craig Tomashoff and Jeannie Park, "Philly's Flip, Hip Will Smith Takes On Hollywood . . . ," *People*, September 29, 1990, p. 83.
38. Quoted in Mary Murphy, "Will Smith: Fresh Prince of Bel-Air," *TV Guide*, September 29, 1990, p. 5.
39. Quoted in Murphy, "Rap 'n' Rhyme with the Prince of Prime Time," p. 8.
40. Quoted in Nickson, "Will Smith," p. 51.
41. Quoted in *Jet*, "Will Smith, as Fresh Prince, Uses Christmas Show to Tell How Humor Solves Family Problems," December 23, 1991, p. 58.

Chapter 4: Freshman Movie Actor

42. Quoted in Mike Sager, "Fresh King," *Vibe*, September 1998, p. 136.

43. Quoted in Nickson, "Will Smith," p. 58.
44. Quoted in Nickson, "Will Smith," p. 66.
45. Quoted in Rita Kempley, "Made in America," *Washington Post,* May 28, 1993, p. 13.
46. Quoted in Michael Segell, "Will Smith," *Cosmopolitan,* October 1993, p. 102.
47. Quoted in Fleming, "Will Smith," p. 67.
48. Quoted in Fleming, "Will Smith," p. 67.
49. Quoted in Norment, "Will Smith," p. 34.
50. Quoted in Fleming, "Will Smith," p. 67.
51. Quoted in Norment, "Will Smith," p. 34.
52. Quoted in Michael J. Legeros, review of *Six Degrees of Separation,* n.d., www.us.imdb.com.
53. Quoted in James Berardinelli, review of *Six Degrees of Separation,* December 8, 1993, www. moviereviews.colossus.net.
54. Quoted in Jack Kroll, "The Worm in the Big Apple," *Newsweek,* December 20, 1993, p. 121.

Chapter 5: Action Movie Hero

55. Quoted in Nickson, *Will Smith,* p. 79.
56. Quoted in Robb, *King of Cool,* p. 72.
57. Quoted in Robb, *King of Cool,* p. 75.
58. Quoted in Nickson, *Will Smith,* p. 100.
59. Quoted in Nickson, *Will Smith,* p. 102.
60. Quoted in Sager, "Fresh King," p. 136.
61. Quoted in Allison Samuels and Karen Schoemer, "Box Office Prince," *Newsweek,* July 22, 1996, p. 69.
62. Quoted in Gregory Cerio, "Mr. Smith Goes to Stardom," *People,* July 22, 1996, p. 65.
63. Quoted in Mary Bruno, "Tales from the Set of *Independence Day,*" *Mr. Showbiz,* July 4, 1996. www.mrshowbiz.go.com.
64. Quoted in Cerio, "Mister Smith Goes to Stardom," p. 64.
65. Quoted in *Ebony Man,* "Will Smith," p. 62.
66. Quoted in Robb, *King of Cool,* p. 100.
67. Quoted in Susan Wloszczyna, "Film Conquers with Hip Humor," *USA Today,* December 1, 1998, www.usatoday.com.

Chapter 6: Becoming More Versatile

68. Quoted in Robb, *King of Cool,* p. 110.
69. Quoted in Robb, *King of Cool,* p. 112.

70. Quoted in *Jet*, "Will Smith Runs for His Life in Action Thriller *Enemy of the State*," November 23, 1998, p. 58.
71. Quoted in Collins, "Will Smith," p. 64.
72. Quoted in *Movie/TV News*, "Movie Reviews: *Enemy of the State*," October 20, 1998, www.us.imdb.com.
73. Quoted in Peter Travers, "Enemy of the State," July 29, 1998, www.rollingstone.com.
74. Quoted in Degen Penner, "Knockouts," *InStyle*, December 2001, p. 416.
75. Quoted in Robb, *King of Cool*, p. 105.
76. Quoted in Fleming, "Will Smith," p. 67.
77. Quoted in Robb, *King of Cool*, p. 121.
78. Quoted in Fleming, "Will Smith," p. 72.
79. Quoted in Terry Lawson, "Smith Plays to Spiritual Side as Caddie in *Bagger Vance*," *Detroit Free-Press*, October 29, 2000, www.mercurycenter.com.
80. Quoted in Lawson, "Smith Plays to Spiritual Side as Caddie in *Bagger Vance*."
81. Quoted in Lawson, "Smith Plays to Spiritual Side as Caddie in *Bagger Vance*."
82. Quoted in Peter Travers, "The Legend of Bagger Vance," www.rollingstone.com
83. Quoted in Richard von Busack, "In the Rough," November 2, 2000, www.metroactive.com.
84. Quoted in "Lee Slams Smith for 'Driving Mr. Damon,'" November 10, 2000, www.mrshowbiz.go.com.

Chapter 7: Ali and Beyond

85. Quoted in Sandra Lee, "Just the Two of Us," *Library Talk*, September 2001, p. 47.
86. Quoted in Collins, "Will Smith," p. 65.
87. Quoted in Fred Schruers, "Will Power," *Premiere*, December 2001, p. 63.
88. Quoted in *Jet*, "Will Smith Explains Why He Decided to Play Ali," December 24, 2001, p. 58.
89. Quoted in Jon Saraceno, "Will Smith, the Greatest," *USA Today*, December 21, 2001, p. 1.
90. Quoted in Schruers, "Will Power," p. 12.
91. Quoted in Kym Allison Backer, "The Big Will," December 6, 2001. www.essence.com.

92. Quoted in Saraceno, "Will Smith, the Greatest," p. 4.
93. Quoted in Todd McCarthy, "No Sweat on Mann-made *Ali,*" *Variety,* December 17, 2001, p. 35.
94. Quoted in McCarthy, "No Sweat on Mann-made *Ali,*" p. 41.
95. Quoted in Leah Rozen, "Ali," *People,* December 24, 2001, p. 31.
96. Quoted in Peter Travers, "Ali," *Rolling Stone,* January 17, 2002, www.rollingstone.com.
97. Quoted in Saraceno, "Will Smith, the Greatest," p. 1.
98. Quoted in *Prime Time* interview, ABC, December 13, 2001.
99. Quoted in Degen Penner, "Knockouts," p. 412.
100. Quoted in "Russell Simmons," June 13, 2001, www.mtv.com.
101. Quoted in Sager, "The Fresh King," p. 136.

Important Dates in the Life of Will Smith

1968
Willard C. Smith II is born on September 25, 1968, in Philadelphia, Pennsylvania.

1979
Will hears "Rapper's Delight" and gets excited about rap music.

1986
Will meets Jeff Townes, and DJ Jazzy Jeff and the Fresh Prince are born; they have a hit rap music single "Girls Ain't Nothing But Trouble"; Will graduates from high school.

1987
The rap album *Rock the House* is released.

1988
The album *He's the DJ, I'm the Rapper* is released.

1989
DJ Jazzy Jeff and the Fresh Prince win the first Grammy ever given for Best Rap Performance for their "Parents Just Don't Understand"; Will finds out he's bankrupt; his album *And in This Corner* is released.

1990
Will goes to Hollywood and lands the lead in the TV show *Fresh Prince of Bel-Air;* it will run for the next six years.

1991
Album *Homebase* is released; Will and Jeff win second Grammy for the single "Summertime."

1992

Will marries Sheree Zampino; Will's first movie, *Where the Day Takes You,* is released; Willard C. Smith III is born; Will gets Golden Globe nomination for *The Fresh Prince of Bel-Air.*

1993

Album *Code Red* is released; Will's movies *Made in America* and *Six Degrees of Separation* are released.

1994

Will becomes executive producer of *The Fresh Prince of Bel-Air.*

1995

Movie *Bad Boys* is released; divorced from Sheree Zampino.

1996

Independence Day is a huge box-office success on its Fourth of July weekend opening; the final episode of *The Fresh Prince of Bel-Air* is aired; Will and Martin Lawrence get MTV Movie Award nomination for *Bad Boys;* Will begins to date Jada Pinkett.

1997

Men in Black (movie) is released and tops the summer box office for the year; "Men in Black" (recording) tops the *Billboard* Hot 100 Singles Airplay chart for four weeks; Will wins Blockbuster Entertainment Awards for *Independence Day* (movie) and for "Men in Black" (soundtrack). He also wins MTV Movie Awards for best screen kiss (with Vivica Fox) and best song for a film *(Men in Black)*; Will signs contract with Columbia for more rap records; his album *Big Willie Style* is his first under the name Will Smith rather than as the Fresh Prince; he marries Jada Pinkett.

1998

The movie *Enemy of the State* is released; son Jaden Christopher Syre Smith is born; "Gettin' Jiggy Wit It" is the longest-running top single record of the year; "Men in Black" wins Grammy for Best Rap Solo performance; Will establishes Overbrook Entertainment to produce films and records.

1999

Movie *Wild Wild West* is released and hammered by the critics, but the title track from the movie tops the Hot 100; Will wins his fourth Grammy for "Gettin' Jiggy Wit It"; album *Willennium* is released and quickly makes the Top 10.

2000

Movie *The Legend of Bagger Vance* is released and Spike Lee criticizes Will for taking a role that ignores racism. Will is nominated for Grammy ("Wild Wild West") and he performs at the awards show, but he comes home empty-handed; the movie *Wild Wild West* is "awarded" five Golden Raspberry Awards; Will's third child, a girl named Willow Camille Reign Smith, is born.

2001

Will spends most of the year working on the movie *Ali,* including a trip to Africa; his rap record "Just the Two of Us" becomes a picture book and earns rave reviews; *Ali* is released and does well on its opening weekend.

2002

Will is nominated for an Academy Award for portraying Muhammad Ali in *Ali; Men in Black 2* is released.

For Further Reading

Books

Sherry Ayazai-Hashjin, *Rap and Hip Hop: The Voice of a Generation.* New York: Rosen, 1999. A primer on the history and development of this cultural phenomenon.

Mark Bego, *Will Smith: The Freshest Prince.* Kansas City, MO: Andrews McMeel, 1998. A light and breezy overview of Smith's life with pictures on most pages.

Maggie Marron, *Will Smith: From Rap Star to Mega Star.* New York: Warner Books, 2000. A brief outline of Smith's life with full-page pictures and several trivia quizzes.

Stacy Stauffer, *Will Smith.* Philadelphia: Chelsea House, 1998. A slightly more thorough look at the actor's life.

Works Consulted

Books

Quincy Jones, *Q.* New York: Doubleday, 2001. A complete look at the life of a multitalented black pioneer in the entertainment business.

Chris Nickson, *Will Smith.* New York: St. Martin's, 1999. A paperback rich in the stories behind the facts of Smith's life.

Brian J. Robb, *King of Cool: Will Smith.* London: Plexus Publishing, 2000. An authoritative account of the facts of Smith's life that includes full color pictures.

K.S. Rodriguez, *Will Smith: From Fresh Prince to King of Cool.* New York: Harper-Collins, 1998. Covers the early years in good detail.

Earl L. Stewart, *African-American Music: An Introduction.* New York: Wadsworth, 1998. Covers black music from ancient Africa to rap with a good chapter on the roots of rap.

Periodicals

Rachel Abramowitz, "Queen Bee," *Us Weekly,* October 2000.

Harry Allen, "Hip Hop Madness," *Essence,* April 1989.

American Visions, "Why Not Just Laugh at Ourselves," April 1993.

David Ansen, "Cool Film About a Hot Man," *Newsweek,* December 24, 2001.

Meredith Berkman, "Can Will Smith Play on Park Avenue?" *Entertainment,* December 24, 1993.

John Brodie, "The Contender," *GQ,* December 2001.

C.L. Brown, "Film's Accuracy Scores Big with Panel," *Courier Journal,* December 21, 2001.

Jeryl Brunner, "Will Smith," *InStyle,* August 2001.

Gregory Cerio, "Mister Smith Goes to Stardom," *People,* September 22, 1996.

Gordon Chambers and Joan Morgan, "Droppin' Knowledge: A Rap Roundtable," *Essence,* September 1992.

Nancy Collins, "Will Smith," *Rolling Stone,* December 1, 1998.

John Dempsey, "TBS Grabs Fresh Prince," *Variety,* December 18, 1995.

Ebony Man, "Will Smith," April 1994.

Ebony, "Will Smith," August 1996.

Audrey Edwards, "Will Smith," *Essence,* May 1998.

Michael Fleming, "Will Smith," *Playboy,* December 2001.

Joe Flint, "On the Air," *Entertainment Weekly,* September 11, 1997.

Vern G. Gaye, "TV Networks 'Colorize' More Programs," *Emerge,* September 1993.

Geoff Gordon, "Six Degrees of Trepidation," *The Advocate,* February 8, 1994.

Deborah Gregory, "Black and White and In Color," *Essence,* October 1992.

Zondra Hughes, Joy Bennett Kinnon, and Glenn Jeffers, "The Greatest," *Ebony,* 2002.

Jet, "How Will Smith Crossed Over from Hit Rapper to Hot Actor," January 27, 1997.

Jet, "Hubert-Whitten Sues NBC; Charges . . . ," *Jet,* January 10, 1994.

Jet, "Rap Star Finds TV Fame as 'Fresh Prince of Bel Air,'" October 3, 1990.

Jet, "Will Smith, as Fresh Prince, Uses Christmas Show to Tell How Humor Solves Family Problems," December 23, 1991.

Jet, "Will Smith Explains Why He Decided to Play 'Ali' in New Movie," December 24.

Jet, "Will Smith Runs for His Life in Action Thriller *Enemy of the State,*" November 23, 1998.

Dave Karger and Mark Harris, "Golden Opportunities," *Entertainment Weekly,* January 18, 2002.

Rita Kempley, "Made in America," *Washington Post,* May 28, 1993.

Kevin Koffler, "Fresh Prince," *Seventeen,* July 1992.

Jack Kroll, "The Worm in the Big Apple," *Newsweek,* December 20, 1993.

Susan Lambert, "Will Smith Saves the World," www.boxoff.com.

Library Talk, "Just the Two of Us," September 2001.

A. Light, "In the Studio," *Rolling Stone,* April 4, 1991.

Todd McCarthy, "No Sweat on Mann-made *Ali,*" *Variety,* December 17, 2001.

Sharon Moshavi, "Viewers Needed," *Forbes,* September 5, 1993.

Mary Murphy, "Rap 'n' Rhyme with the Prince of Prime Time," *TV Guide,* October 13, 1990.

Mary Murphy, "Will Smith: Fresh Prince of Bel-Air," *TV Guide,* September 29, 1990.

Chris Nashawaty, "Inspired Larceny of a Former Fresh Prince," *Fortune,* December 20, 1999.

Lynn Norment, "Will Smith," *Ebony,* August 1996.

Ralph Novak, "Bad Boys," *People,* April 24, 1995.

Andy Pawelczak, "Six Degrees of Separation," *Films in Review,* May 1994.

Degen Penner, "Knockouts," *InStyle,* December 2001.

People, "The Fresh Prince of Bel-Air," June 26, 2000.

People, "Jazzy Jeff and Fresh Prince Rap's More Mild Than Wild Guys," October 3, 1988.

People, "Will Smith," May 11, 1998.

Laura B. Randolph, "The Real-Life Fresh Prince of Bel-Air," *Ebony,* April 1991.

Jeffrey Ressner, "No Nightmares for D.J. Jazzy Jeff and the Fresh Prince," *Rolling Stone,* December 1, 1988.

Jeffrey Ressner, "Raps to Riches," *Rolling Stone,* September 20, 1990.

J.R. Reynolds, "'Fresh Prince' a Watershed for Hip-Hop," *Billboard,* September 24, 1994.

David Ritz, "Will Power," *Essence,* February 1993.

Lea Rozen, "Ali," *People,* December 24, 2001.

Mike Sager, "The Fresh King," *Vibe,* September 1998.

Allison Samuels and Karen Schoemer, "Box Office Prince," *Newsweek,* July 22, 1996.

Jon Saraceno, "Will Smith, the Greatest," *USA Today,* December 21, 2001.

Karen Schoemer, "His Future's So Bright," *Newsweek,* July 7, 1997.

Fred Schruers, "Will Power," *Premiere,* December 2001.

Michael Segell, "Will Smith," *Cosmopolitan,* October 1993.

Francelia Sevin, "A Talk with Will Smith," *Scholastic Update,* September 6, 1991.

Shawnee Smith, "Columbia Thinks 'Big' for Smith," *Billboard,* November 8, 1997.

Mia Sulphor, "Mr. Smith Goes to Harlem with His Ali Shuffle," *Us Weekly,* April 23, 2001.

Chuck Taylor, "Ali Is More Than Daydreamin' as She Charts Her Career Path," *Billboard,* September 12, 1998.

Malissa Thompson, "Will Smith Gets Fresh with Jazzy Jeff," *Seventeen,* December 1993.

Craig Tomashoff, "Talking with Will Smith," *People,* December 7, 1998.

Craig Tomashoff and Jeannie Park, "Philly's Flip, Hip Will Smith Takes On Hollywood," *People,* September 29, 1990.

Alex Tresniowski, "Mr. Smith Takes a Bride," *People,* January 1, 1998.

Us Weekly, "Ali," December 24, 2001.

Alex Wolff, "Julius Erving," *Sports Illustrated,* September 19, 1994.

Ting Yu, "Mr. Smith Goes to Barnes and Noble," *People,* November 20, 2000.

Internet Sources

"A Couple of Real Fighters," June 12, 2001, www.calendarlive.com.

Kym Allison Backer, "The Big Will," www.essence.com.

James Berardinelli, "Six Degrees of Separation," December 8, 1993, www.moviereviews.colossus.net.

"Boomin' Back! Pumping It Up with Jazzy Jeff and Fresh Prince," www.members.austarmetro.com.

Sandra Brennan, "Stockard Channing Biography," www.movies.yahoo.com

Mary Bruno, ed. "Tales from the Set of *Independence Day,*" July 4, 1996. www.mrshowbiz.go.com.

Ebony Man, Will Smith, September 1996, www.fulltext.asp.

"Grisham Rejects Will Smith," www.us.imbd.com.

Brian Hiatt, "LL Cool J, Ja Rule Hear Farrakhan Challenge Rap Community," June 13, 2001, www.mtv.com.

"I Enjoy Life . . . ," www.mrshowbiz.go.com.

Anne Janette Johnson, "Personal Information," *Contemporary Musicians,* June 1991, vol. 5, www.members.austarmetro.com.

Terry Lawson, "Smith Plays to Spiritual Side as a Caddie in *Bagger Vance,*" www.0.mercurycenter.com.

Michael J. Legeros, "Six Degrees of Separation," www.us.imdb.com.

"Leo Slams Smith for 'Driving Mr. Damon,'" September 10, 2000, www.mr showbiz.go.com.

"Ian McKellen," www.cucare.com.

"Men in Black—Sequel Changed," January 9, 2001, www.empireonly.co.uk.

"Movie Reviews: *Enemy of the State,"* Movie/TV News, www.us.imbd.com.

Rick Schultz, "Prince Charming," www.mrshowbiz.go.com.

"Taking on Ali," www.abcnews.go.com.

Peter Travers, "Ali," Rolling Stone, January 17, 2002. www.rollingstone.com.

Peter Travers, "Enemy of the State," www.rollingstone.com.

Peter Travers, "The Legend of Bagger Vance," www.rollingstone.com.

Kenneth Turan, "Movie Review: *Bad Boys,*" www.calendarlive.com.

Richard von Busack, "In the Rough," www.metroactive.com.

Jon A. Webb, "Six Degrees of Separation," 1993, www.us.imdb.com.

Wild Wild West, www.us.imdb.com.

"Wild Wild West Goes Up in Flames," September 3, 1998, www.mrshow biz.go.com.

"Will Smith and Martin Lawrence Prepare for *Bad Boys* Sequel," www.us. imdb.com.

"Will Smith for President?" November 19, 1999, www.mrshowbiz.go.com.

"Will Smith: I've Had Enough of Playing Icons," March 5, 2002, www.us. imbd.com.

"Will Smith's Close Encounters with Female Fans," November 11, 1996, www.mrshowbiz.go.com.

"Will Smith Starts Producing," November 12, 1997, www.mrshowbiz.go.com.

"Will Smith Sued for Libel," August 21, 1997, www.mrshowbiz.go.com.

Susan Wloszczyna, "Film Conquers with Hip Humor," *USA Today,* www.usa today.com.

Radio and Television

Terry Gross, "Interview with Russell Simmons," *Fresh Air,* November 27, 2001 (PBS Radio).

TV Interviews with Smith: *Prime Time,* December 13, 2001;
Jay Leno, December 17, 2001;
Early Show, December 21 and 24, 2001;
Regis and Kelly, December 21, 2001;
Early Show, December 24, 2001.

Index

93

Picture Credits

About the Author

Marilyn D. Anderson is the author of seventeen children's chapter books, one picture book, four nonfiction books for children, a children's play, and numerous magazine stories and articles for both children and adults. Before becoming a professional writer, Anderson taught bands and choirs in Minnesota, Vermont, and Indiana. She and her husband currently live in Bedford, Indiana. Her hobbies include showing dressage horses, appearing in plays, and conducting her church choir.